A Thousand Splendid Suns

(PLAY SCRIPT)

A Thousand Splendid Suns

(PLAY SCRIPT)

ADAPTED BY **URSULA RANI SARMA**

BASED ON THE NOVEL BY **KHALED HOSSEINI**

RIVERHEAD BOOKS

NEW YORK

2018

RIVERHEAD BOOKS
An imprint of
Penguin Random House LLC
375 Hudson Street
New York, New York 10014

A Thousand Splendid Suns was first performed on February 1, 2017,
at American Conservatory Theater's Geary Theater in San Francisco.

This play is adapted from the novel *A Thousand Splendid Suns* by Khaled Hosseini
(Riverhead Books, 2007).
Copyright © 2007 by ATSS Publications, LLC.

Library of Congress Cataloging-in-Publication Data

Names: Sarma, Ursula Rani, author. | Hosseini, Khaled. Thousand splendid suns.
Title: A thousand splendid suns (the play script): based on the novel by
Khaled Hosseini / adapted by Ursula Rani Sarma.
Description: New York: Riverhead Books, 2018.
Identifiers: LCCN 2017026341 (print) | LCCN 2017030277 (ebook) |
ISBN 9780525534471 (eBook) | ISBN 9780735218246 (trade paperback)
Subjects: LCSH: Families—Afghanistan—Drama.
Classification: LCC PR6119.A76 (ebook) |
LCC PR6119.A76 T49 2018 (print) | DDC 822/.92—c23
LC record available at https://lccn.loc.gov/2017026341
p.   cm.

Printed in the United States of America
1   3   5   7   9   10   8   6   4   2

Book design by Gretchen Achilles

A THOUSAND SPLENDID SUNS

KHALED HOSSEINI was born in Kabul, Afghanistan, and moved to the United States in 1980. He is the author of the *New York Times* bestsellers *The Kite Runner*, *A Thousand Splendid Suns*, and *And the Mountains Echoed*. He is a U.S. Goodwill Envoy to the United Nations Refugee Agency and the founder of the Khaled Hosseini Foundation, a nonprofit that provides humanitarian assistance to the people of Afghanistan.

URSULA RANI SARMA is an internationally acclaimed writer of Irish Indian descent. She has written fifteen plays for companies such as the Abbey Theatre in Dublin, the Royal National Theatre in London, the American Conservatory Theater in San Francisco, the Traverse Theatre in Edinburgh, Paines Plough Theatre in London, Clean Break in London, and BBC Radio, among many others. Some of these plays include the award-winning *The Dark Things*, *The Spider Men*, *The Magic Tree*, and a new version of Federico García Lorca's *Yerma*. Her work for the screen includes projects for the BBC, Film4, RTÉ, TV3, and Sky. She has received numerous awards and has held writer-in-residence positions for the Royal National Theatre in London, the Eugene O'Neill Theater Center in Connecticut, and Paines Plough Theatre in London.

A Thousand Splendid Suns

(PLAY SCRIPT)

Note on casting: the play can be done with a cast of eight adults and two children.

CHARACTERS

Laila

Mariam

Young Mariam

Nana, Mariam's mother

Jalil, Mariam's father

Tariq

Babi, Laila's father

Fariba, Laila's mother

Mullah Faizullah, Mariam's teacher

Rasheed, Mariam and Laila's husband

Aziza, Laila's daughter

Zalmai, Laila's son

Driver

Militiaman

Interrogator

Doctor

Nurse

Talib soldier

Abdul Sharif

Wakil

Zaman

Act One

SCENE ONE

Lights up on Babi, a slight man in his forties with glasses. He is reading from a brown leather-bound book. At his feet sits Laila, fifteen, listening attentively. They are both surrounded by books, boxes, and clothes. 1992.

BABI: How beautiful is Kabul nestled beneath her barren mountains

Even the Rose is wanton for her silken thorns

Though the wind, heavy with her fine and powdered soil, stings my eyes

I love her, for knowledge and love are both born of this earth . . .

We hear a woman's voice call out.

FARIBA: Hakim!

Babi and Laila exchange a look, then he continues to read. A soft whine begins.

BABI: I sing to praise her glorious blooms

I blush in wonder at the beauty of her trees—

Fariba, forty, enters. She is a tired, brokenhearted woman and it shows.

FARIBA: Hakim! Now is not the time for poetry.

BABI: There is always time for poetry, Fariba.

FARIBA: And when the taxi comes and we're not ready, what then? Will poetry get us to Pakistan? Will it carry us all the way there?

LAILA: Oh, leave him be, Mammy. *(The whine gets louder.)*

BABI: It's okay, Laila, your mother is right, we have no time . . .

Babi exits back into their house. The whine gets louder still. Both Laila and Fariba stop to listen as it becomes the whistle of an incoming missile. It increases in volume as it approaches and then passes by overhead, detonating somewhere in the distance. Fariba returns to sorting clothes and boxes almost immediately.

LAILA: It's the whistling I hate, not knowing where it's going to land . . .

FARIBA: Just be happy it wasn't here.

LAILA: But it landed somewhere, someone in the city is now dead. Look, there's the smoke . . . I heard if they don't move the bodies in time, then the dogs start to eat them—

FARIBA: Hush now, no point in talking like this, keep sorting, the taxi will be here soon.

Laila pulls her mother's wedding dress from a pile and stares at it in shock.

LAILA: Mammy . . . you're not selling your wedding dress?

FARIBA: It's heavy and we can get some money for it.

LAILA: But it's beautiful . . .

FARIBA: Beauty won't put food on our plates; what do you think will feed us when we get to Peshawar? Put it in the pile . . . *(Babi enters with a box of books. He selects two, then puts one back, then takes another.)* It's your father you should feel sorry for . . . having to leave all his precious books behind . . . look at him . . . in agony . . .

BABI: It's like that game . . . you're going to a desert island and you can only bring five books, which ones would you choose? You never think you will actually have to do it . . .

LAILA: Poor Babi, can I help?

BABI: *(overwhelmed)* I have six more boxes inside . . . perhaps it's better to leave them all behind.

LAILA: How about I choose for you? I'll put them in a bag and you won't open it until we get settled?

BABI: Thank you, Laila . . . but some things people just have to do for themselves . . . *(Babi exiting.)* No time . . . we have no time . . .

FARIBA: When I met him my friends would say, "Hakim may not be the best for mending a fence, but if you have a book that needs urgent reading, then he's your man." *(Laila laughs.)* I don't know why you're laughing, you're the very same.

LAILA: I can fix things, I fixed the screen.

FARIBA: Yes, but you're a thinker, a dreamer, not like your brothers, they were fighters. *(Beat. She looks back toward the house.)* I have spent so many days inside this house . . . listening to the ticking of the clock . . . thinking of all the minutes, the days and years spread out before me. All of it without them.

LAILA: Mammy, don't . . .

FARIBA: *(looks to Laila, touches her face)* But at least I still have you, eh? *(Laila smiles and goes to move her face away, but Fariba has seen something, turns her face back to hers, examines it.)* Laila . . . are you plucking your eyebrows?

LAILA: *(self-conscious)* Just a little.

FARIBA: When did you become a young woman?

LAILA: I don't know . . . it just happened, I guess.

BABI: *(enters with another box of books)* Maybe we will catch up with Tariq and his family when we get to Peshawar. They left what? Ten days ago now? What do you think, Laila?

LAILA: *(nonchalant)* Maybe.

FARIBA: Look at her, pretending not to care.

LAILA: I didn't say I didn't care.

FARIBA: Well, it's time he did something about the situation, right, Hakim? How old is Tariq?

Babi exits again.

LAILA: Seventeen.

FARIBA: It was one thing when you were little kids running around, but now things are different . . . and remember, he is a boy so he doesn't care about reputation, but you are a girl and a pretty one at that. Your reputation is a delicate thing. Like a mynah bird in your hands, loosen your grip and away it flies.

LAILA: He's like a brother to me.

FARIBA: *(furious)* That he is not, you will not liken that one-legged carpenter's boy to your brothers. There is no one like them. You don't remember, you were too young when they went off to fight, but they were real men . . . heroes, Laila.

LAILA: Yes, Mammy, I know.

FARIBA: All I'm saying is if you're not careful, people will talk . . . *(Babi reenters with another box of books.)* Isn't that right, Hakim? Tariq should ask for her hand . . .

BABI: Oh, boys can wait, Laila can be anything she wants . . . *(To Laila)* Things weren't always like they are now; here in Kabul women taught at the university, they ran schools, held office in the government. These days will come again—

FARIBA: And where will we be then? Long gone.

BABI: *(upset by this, turning to her)* Don't you think it's hard for me too? I've spent most of my life here in Kabul, it's all I know . . .

Laila looks at them, afraid for a minute this might all fall apart.

FARIBA: *(softer now, tender almost)* Then both our hearts are broken . . . but what can we do? *(Beat. She Stands stiffly.)* That's everything.

BABI: We're going to need a second taxi to take all this to the pawnshop.

FARIBA: I'll go and prepare the lunch, come in and eat when you are done here . . . *(Beat. To Laila)* Don't let him weep too long over his books . . .

Laila watches Babi reading again from the book where he read the poem. Laila goes to him and takes the book.

LAILA: Let me . . . *(She reads. Babi begins to pack his books away, pausing moments later, listening intently.)*

Every street of Kabul entices my eyes

Through the bazaars I watch the caravans of Egypt pass by

I could not count the moons that shimmer on her roofs

And the thousand splendid suns that hide behind her walls . . .

And I, I sing to the gardens of Jahanara, of Sharhara

Even the choirs of heaven cry out for their emerald pastures.

Laila looks up to see Babi is sobbing.

Oh, Babi, we'll come back. When this war is over, we'll come back to Kabul, you'll see . . .

BABI: *(sets the books down at his feet, heartbroken)* You choose for me, Laila, I cannot . . .

Babi enters the house and Laila begins to go through the books, looking at the titles. In the distance a low whine begins.

FARIBA: *(from offstage)* Laila, come and eat . . .

LAILA: I'm coming . . .

She picks up more books, worries she will make the wrong choice and her father will be disappointed. The whine gets louder and louder and turns into a whistle. Laila recognizes it and looks up, as though she might see it approaching. As it gets louder, she puts her hand over her eyes as if to shield them. Then the giant roar of an explosion and a blinding flash of white before a sudden and ink-black darkness. Laila's silhouette is burned into our eyes.

SCENE TWO

Laila is now on the ground on a makeshift bed. Mariam, midthirties and worn out, stands above her with a glass of water. 1992.

MARIAM: Do you know who I am? *(Laila begins to moan. Mariam offers her the glass of water, a pill to swallow.)* Here, swallow this, it will help with the pain . . . *(She helps Laila swallow the pill.)* I am Rasheed's wife, we live around the corner from your house. You've been very ill . . . you almost died in fact . . .

LAILA: Where . . . where is my father?

MARIAM: A shell hit your house . . .

LAILA: *(beat)* My mother?

MARIAM: Rasheed pulled you from the rubble, no one else survived . . . do you remember?

Laila begins to sob. She shakes. Mariam knows she needs comforting but not how to do it. Rasheed enters, carrying a new pillow and blanket. He is delighted to see Laila is awake, giddy almost.

RASHEED: You're awake, that's good, that's very good, and how are you feeling? We heard the shell fall . . . our walls shook with the blast. I dug you out with my own hands. There was a piece of metal this long in your shoulder . . . but you're all right now.

LAILA: My parents?

MARIAM: I already told her.

RASHEED: I'm so very sorry . . . there was nothing to be done . . . I managed to save some of your father's books . . . most were burned in the blaze or looted, but not all . . . no, not all . . . *(Laila takes this in, in shock, struggling to absorb. Rasheed looks to Mariam, who shrugs.)* I've just been to the market and look what I bought for you . . . a new pillow . . . blanket . . . vitamins . . . for you . . . *(He holds them out to her; she doesn't respond. Rasheed hands them to Laila. He sits down on his haunches, addresses Laila gently.)* You survived. That's something, eh? *(Beat.)* . . . Now rest . . . I got fresh meat for your meal . . . you need all the iron you can get . . . and some *halwa* . . .

LAILA: I'm not hungry.

RASHEED: But you must eat . . . how else are you to get better? Don't you worry about anything, we will take care of you now.

Rasheed leaves. Mariam begins to place the new pillow and blanket around her.

LAILA: I have a friend, he will come for me, can your husband try to reach him?

MARIAM: What is his name?

LAILA: Tariq, Mohammad Tariq Walizai, his family will take me in, I know they will.

MARIAM: I'll ask him . . . rest now.

Mariam leaves. Laila is still in shock, in grief, eyes closed.

LAILA: Tariq . . .

The lighting state changes as we transition to a dream/memory, ghostly almost. Suddenly Tariq appears. He's a gentle boy with one prosthetic leg and a very sweet smile. 1989.

TARIQ: Where's my welcome home?

LAILA: *(delighted to see him)* You were gone for ages . . . *(She can hardly contain herself. She thumps him on the arm playfully.)*

TARIQ: My uncle was sick.

LAILA: Your hair . . .

TARIQ: You like it? You want to feel? *(He bends his head for her to touch. There is a moment here; she is aware of the sensation of her hand on him.)* So what did I miss?

LAILA: Nothing, same old things, nothing new.

TARIQ: How is your mother?

LAILA: Some good days, some bad. The same. She stays in bed, sleeps, waits for my brothers to come home . . .

TARIQ: And your father?

LAILA: Also the same, happy with his books . . . *(Beat.)* Hey, I have one, what goes round the world but stays in a corner?

TARIQ: A stamp.

LAILA: You heard it before?

TARIQ: No, I just figured it out. Let's go to the zoo.

LAILA: Liar . . . you already heard it.

TARIQ: You're just jealous because I'm so smart.

LAILA: Don't make me laugh . . . have you ever beaten me at chess?

TARIQ: I let you win.

LAILA: And who do you call on to help with your math homework even though you're a year ahead?

TARIQ: Math is boring. Now, are we going to the zoo or not?

LAILA: *(laughs)* Yes, we're going.

TARIQ: Good.

LAILA: *(beat, giddy, so delighted he is back)* I missed you.

TARIQ: *(taken aback, awkward, not sure how to take it)* What's the matter with you? Did you fall and hit your head?

LAILA: *(faltering, then recovering)* It was a joke . . . I was joking . . . just wanted to annoy you . . .

TARIQ: Well, it worked . . .

LAILA: Well, good . . .

An awkward pause, then each steals a shy glance of the other. Laila is thinking desperately of something to break the silence.

Hasina's mother wants to marry her off to her cousin in Lahore. She says he eats with his mouth open, she did an im-
pression of him, it was so funny Giti almost choked on her
halwa, we were thumping her on the back for ages.

TARIQ: She's too young.

LAILA: Her mother says she's not.

TARIQ: Well, I'm never getting married.

LAILA: *(steals a look at him, a little disappointed)* Me neither.

TARIQ: Weddings are stupid.

LAILA: All the fuss.

TARIQ: And the money.

LAILA: For what?

TARIQ: For clothes you'll never wear again . . . *(Laila laughs at
this; it's a little forced.)* If I ever do get married, they will have
to make room for three on the wedding stage. Me, the bride,
and the guy holding a gun to my head . . . anyway, are we
going to the zoo or not?

LAILA: We're going . . . just let me . . . *(She turns to get her head
scarf, and when she looks back Tariq is gone; the lighting state
reverts as she sinks backward into the bed.)*

*Lights down on Laila and up on the next room where Rasheed is lis-
tening to his radio, smoking.*

MARIAM: How long is she staying?

RASHEED: Until she is better. Poor thing. You get her whatever
she needs.

Mariam stares at him for a moment, not trusting him. Rasheed looks up.

MARIAM: She has a friend . . . someone who will come for her.

RASHEED: Who? That lame boy? What can he do for her?

MARIAM: She says he will take care of her.

RASHEED: He's a cripple, he can't even take care of himself. A young girl like that needs proper protection, especially the way the country is now that the Soviets have left; there are violent, reckless men roaming the streets . . .

MARIAM: Then what will I tell her?

RASHEED: *(looks away now, avoids her gaze)* Tell her I will do what's best for her . . .

Mariam watches him, a hint of dread; she suspects what he has in mind.

Passage of time illustrated by Mariam following a cycle of chores. Laila gradually becomes stronger; she rises from her bed and goes to a basin of water. She partially undresses and begins to wash herself, literally washing the blood from her arms and shoulders. There is something arresting in this image, sensuality without intention. Rasheed enters and watches her; he can't help himself, he cannot look away. Through-out all this Mariam follows her cycle of chores, faltering only when she observes Rasheed's gaze on Laila, understanding what is happening before her eyes.

SCENE THREE

The sound of shelling in the distance. It's unbearably hot. Mariam moves about the room, cleaning. Laila stands in the doorway watching her. Laila has a letter in her hands. 1992.

LAILA: It's so hot . . . I can't breathe . . . *(No answer from Mariam.)* Don't you find it hot? *(Still no answer. Beat. She shuffles uncomfortably.)* I've written another letter, to my friend's uncle in Peshawar, you think your husband will send it for me? It's been six weeks since he left so he should be there by now. *(Mariam ignores her.)* Thank you for looking after me, I know I owe you my life . . . *(Mariam ignores her.)* Have I done something to offend you? Tell me and I won't do it again . . .

Rasheed enters.

RASHEED: Laila, you have a visitor.

LAILA: *(delighted)* Tariq?

RASHEED: Cover yourselves. Mariam, make tea.

Rasheed exits while the two women cover their heads with their scarves. Rasheed enters now with Abdul Sharif. Laila rushes to meet him, then stops, disappointed.

LAILA: Where is he?

RASHEED: Laila, this is Abdul Sharif. Mariam, bring the tea, sit please . . .

ABDUL SHARIF: Thank you, thank you . . . I'm still *(coughs dramatically)* recovering . . . five more days of pills to go . . . so you are Laila?

LAILA: Yes . . . did you know my parents?

ABDUL SHARIF: No, no . . . *(Mariam brings tea.)* Thank you, *hamshira* . . . no, I am a businessman . . . I have stores here in Kabul and in Peshawar . . . I was there recently visiting my family and I became quite ill . . . *(He coughs again.)* The doctor said I had blood poisoning, he said two or three more days and I would have made my wife a widow . . . *(He pauses for effect, sees Laila is not interested.)* They put me in the intensive-care unit, and that, *hamshira*, that is where I met your friend, Mohammad Tariq Walizai.

LAILA: Tariq . . . *(Throughout the remainder of this scene Laila implodes internally.)*

ABDUL SHARIF: He had been in a truck full of refugees headed for Peshawar when the rocket hit. Most of them died instantly. Tariq was in the bed next to mine, he was burned, badly burned, and heavily drugged. *(Laila takes an intake of breath.)* But sometimes he spoke, about where he had lived, his mother, his father . . . but mostly about you, *hamshira*. I could tell he cared a great deal for you . . . *(Beat.)* I woke up one night and there were doctors huddled about his bed, alarms bleeping, syringes everywhere . . . *(Beat.)* The nurse said he fought valiantly . . .

Mariam is shocked, looks at Laila.

MARIAM: He is dead?

ABDUL SHARIF: I'm afraid so, *hamshira*. *(To Laila)* I'm sorry to be the bearer of bad news . . . but I thought you should know . . .

Laila exits to her room, in shock and still frozen. Rasheed lets Abdul Sharif out, then returns to where Mariam is waiting for him anxiously.

MARIAM: *(beat, watching him)* I know what you're thinking.

RASHEED: And what is that?

MARIAM: That you will take her as your second wife.

RASHEED: *(beat, nonchalantly)* So what if I am? It's a common thing and you know it; I have friends who have two, three, and four wives. Think of it this way, I'm giving you help around the house and her a sanctuary. These days a woman needs a husband.

MARIAM: Eighteen years I never asked you for anything. Not one thing. I'm asking now.

RASHEED: We need to legitimize the situation, people will talk. It looks dishonorable for a young unmarried woman to be living here like this. It's bad for my reputation, and hers, and yours I might add.

MARIAM: She's too young.

RASHEED: She's fifteen, hardly a child, you were fifteen, remember? My mother was fourteen when she had me, thirteen when she married.

Mariam pauses, tries to contain her rage.

MARIAM: I don't want this.

RASHEED: It's not about what you want.

MARIAM: I'm too old for you to do this to me.

RASHEED: Don't be so dramatic, she's too young, you're too old, it's nonsense.

MARIAM: I won't allow it.

Rasheed sneers at her.

RASHEED: You want me to kick her out instead? How far would she get with no food, no water, no money, bullets and rockets flying everywhere? How many days do you suppose she will last before she is abducted, raped, tossed into a roadside ditch with her throat slit? Or all three? Or she could keep warm in a brothel maybe, business is booming there I hear. A beauty like hers ought to bring in a small fortune, don't you think? *(He sees the hurt in Mariam and stops himself, calmer now, reasoning.)* Look, I knew you wouldn't take this well and I don't really blame you. But think of it this way, she can't continue to stay here like this and she has nowhere else to go. This is for the best, Mariam.

Rasheed turns and walks into Laila's room, where she is lying on the bed. He watches her for a moment; he feels vulnerable suddenly. He desperately wants this girl to see him the way he sees her.

I know a thing or two about loss . . . *(Laila doesn't respond.)* My first wife died in childbirth, I was in the next room and I could hear her cries, but the women wouldn't let me in . . . It was no place for a man, they said, but where else should a man be other than beside his wife as she is dying? *(Laila looks up now, listening. Rasheed waits a moment; this is difficult for him.)* And then my son . . . my beautiful boy . . . he was taken from me too . . . drowned in a lake . . . when he was only four years old. *(Beat. This has huge weight for him still.)* Since he died, there has been no light in my life, Laila, not until now . . . *(Laila wipes the tears from her cheeks, knows where this is going now.)* And all paths lead somewhere . . . I know that you will need some time to consider but . . . I would do right by you . . . I would protect you always . . . *(Beat.)* If you were my wife . . . *(Laila says nothing. Rasheed takes Babi's book in his hands.)* You know your father, God give him peace, your father and I used to have discussions all the time, about books and politics, all the time. It makes sense that you have come to be here, don't you think? *(Laila doesn't answer. Rasheed turns to go, half afraid she will say no.)* You can think about it . . . give me your answer when you are ready—

LAILA: *(still staring at the book)* You can have it now . . . *(Beat.)* My answer is yes.

Rasheed is delighted, can hardly believe it. Mariam enters. She stares at Laila throughout the remainder of the scene. Laila is aware of her gaze and is uncomfortable.

RASHEED: *(delighted)* Good . . . that's good . . . well, you will have only the best . . . I know a good tailor who will make you a beautiful dress and you must have flowers . . . lots of flowers. You have a favorite? Daisies? Tulips? Lilacs?

LAILA: I'd rather just . . . get it done . . .

RASHEED: *(smiles, pleased)* Ah good . . . I so hoped you would say that. *(He takes a little box from his pocket and hands it to her. She opens it.)* You like it?

LAILA: Yes . . .

RASHEED: I traded in Mariam's wedding band for it.

LAILA: You traded her ring?

RASHEED: Oh, she doesn't care, she never wore it anyway.

LAILA: No . . . it's not right . . . you should take it back.

RASHEED: *(a flicker of anger which he quickly smothers)* Take it back? I had to add some cash to it, quite a lot in fact, this is a much better ring, twenty-two-karat gold, feel how heavy? See? *(Laila holds the ring, not happy. Rasheed takes it and slips it on her finger.)* See how well it fits? Perfect, just perfect . . .

A choreographed scene where Mariam steps forward and helps to dress Laila for her wedding, adorning her with a beautiful scarf. Rasheed dons a suit jacket as a mullah enters to perform the ceremony. He places Laila's hands in Rasheed's and leaves. Mariam watches Rasheed and

Laila standing together, hands together, then turns and exits. Rasheed begins to undress Laila slowly.

So beautiful . . . the most beautiful thing I've ever seen.

She is almost naked now. Rasheed stares at her; he cannot believe his good fortune. He goes to his knees, pulls her to him. She doesn't move, her arms still by her side. He reaches up for her. Lights down.

SCENE FOUR

Rasheed sits eating. Mariam and Laila stand at either side of him, avoiding eye contact with each other and saying nothing. Rasheed is delighted, giddy even, eyes on his new bride. The tension between Laila and Mariam is obvious. 1992.

RASHEED: What is this? Have I married a pair of statues? Go on, Mariam, say something to her . . . *(Mariam continues to stare into space.)* Though you mustn't blame her, she hasn't got much to say. We are city people, but she is a village girl, she has had no education, she knows nothing of books or politics, not like us. She grew up with her crazy mother in a *kolba* made of mud outside the village. Her father put her there. Have you told her, Mariam? Have you told her you are a *harami*? That your mother hanged herself from a tree? No?

Laila looks at Mariam in shock; she didn't know.

Well, that's who she is, but she is not without qualities. She is sturdy, a good worker, and without pretensions. I'll say it this way: if she were a car she would be a Volga. But you . . . you on the other hand would be a Benz. A brand-new first-class shiny Benz . . . wah, wah . . . *(Beat. He is worried Laila might take offense.)* I'm not saying you are cars, I am just making a point. But one must take certain precautions with a Benz . . . and I am your husband now and it falls on me to guard not only your honor but ours. And you, Laila, you are the queen, the *malika*, and this house is your palace. Anything you need done you ask Mariam and she will do it for you. Won't you, Mariam? And if you fancy something, I will get it for you. You see, that is the sort of husband I am. And all I ask in return is that you avoid leaving this house without my company and that when we are out together you will wear a burqa. Where I come from, it is a man's duty to protect his wife's honor and her reputation and there is something sacred in that. I want to keep you safe, Laila, to protect you, this is how I was raised. Do you understand? *(Beat.)* And Mariam will be my eyes and ears when I am away, not that I am mistrusting. But you are still a young woman, and young women can be prone to mischief. Anyway, Mariam will be accountable and if there is a slipup . . . well . . . on her head be it.

Rasheed stands and walks away, leaving Mariam and Laila at the table. Mariam is barely containing her fury, her pride straining to breaking point.

LAILA: Mariam, please don't think that I—

MARIAM: *(exploding)* I won't be your servant, I won't.

LAILA: No. Of course not.

MARIAM: You may be the palace *malika* and me a *dehati*, but I won't take orders from you. He can slit my throat, but I won't do it, do you hear me? I won't be your servant.

LAILA: No, I don't expect—

MARIAM: If you think you can use your looks to get rid of me, you're wrong. I was here first. I won't be thrown out. I won't have you cast me out.

LAILA: It's not what I want.

MARIAM: I see your wounds are healed up now, you can start doing your share of the housework.

LAILA: Yes, of course . . . and I wanted to thank you for taking care of me.

MARIAM: Well, I wouldn't have fed you and washed you and nursed you if I'd known you were going to turn around and steal my husband.

LAILA: Steal!

MARIAM: And one more thing. I have no use for your company. I don't want it. I want to be left alone and I will return the favor. That's how we will get along.

Mariam turns away.

LAILA: You know I didn't ask for this, for any of this . . .

MARIAM: *(looks at her scathingly)* And you think I did? *(She exits.)*

From offstage Rasheed calls.

RASHEED: Laila!

Laila is frozen, afraid of what he wants. She goes to find Rasheed listening to his radio. He watches her, beckons her closer; she comes. He reaches out for her stomach; she struggles not to recoil. We realize now that Laila is pregnant.

Swelling so quickly, it's going to be a big boy, a Pahlawan like his father . . . *(He gestures to a bag.)* The bag . . . see what's inside . . . *(Laila takes out a little suede winter coat.)* He'll need a coat, the winters here are harsh, we can't have him getting sick.

LAILA: Or her . . .

RASHEED: And we will need to do something about that stove, it's dangerous as it is, and find a new place to keep the knives, little boys are reckless creatures.

LAILA: It may not be a boy . . .

RASHEED: What do you think of Zalmai? It's a good Pashtun name.

LAILA: And if it's a girl?

RASHEED: If it's a girl, and it isn't, but if it is a girl, then you can choose whatever name you want. Do you know how happy you have made me? *(She looks away.)*

And you? Are you happy here? *(Laila doesn't respond.)* Are you?

LAILA: Yes . . .

RASHEED: You have everything you need?

LAILA: Yes . . .

RASHEED: And Mariam? She is making you feel welcome?

LAILA: *(hesitates)* Yes.

Mariam walks in, ignores Rasheed who is oblivious to this memory.

MARIAM: What have you done with my wooden spoon?

LAILA: I didn't touch it, I hardly come into the kitchen.

MARIAM: Yes, I noticed.

LAILA: Is that an accusation? It's what you wanted, you said you would do the meals.

MARIAM: So you're saying it grew little legs and walked out? Teep, teep, teep. Is that what happened?

LAILA: I'm saying maybe you misplaced it.

MARIAM: I've lived in this house for nineteen years, I have kept the spoon in the same drawer since you were shitting your pants.

LAILA: Still it's possible you put it somewhere and forgot.

MARIAM: And it's possible you hid it somewhere just to irritate me.

LAILA: You are a sad and miserable woman.

MARIAM: And you are a whore. A whore and a *dozd*. A thieving whore, that's what you are . . .

Mariam turns and marches off.

A thieving whore!

Rasheed turns to look at Laila.

RASHEED: No fighting then?

LAILA: No, no fighting . . .

RASHEED: Good, good . . .

Lights down. In the kitchen Mariam scrubs dishes. She begins to take her frustration out on them, banging them together. Lights down slowly on her.

SCENE FIVE

In the transition, the banging continues and is accompanied by the crying of a young baby. Mariam still in the kitchen as Rasheed enters, disheveled, cranky. 1993.

RASHEED: It's like someone is ramming a screwdriver into my ear . . . *(He steps on something.)* What the . . . ? *(He looks at it, realizes what it is in disgust.)* You see what this is? *(Mariam barely glances his way.)* It's a shit cloth, I've stepped on a shit cloth, in my own house, in my own home. What is this, a sewer? Can't you keep the place clean at least? *(Mariam struggles to hide her amusement. She continues to cook; the noise of her spoon in the bowl irritates him.)* Can't you stop that? Stop it, I said! *(Mariam stops what she is doing; the baby still wails, winding Rasheed up even more.)* This is torture, that's what this is. I haven't had a decent night's sleep in two months. *(The crying continues as Laila comes through with the baby in her arms on her way to the kitchen.)* Can't you take her outside?

LAILA: She'll catch pneumonia.

RASHEED: It's the middle of the summer.

LAILA: I am not taking her outside!

RASHEED: Sometimes I want to leave that thing in a basket and let her float down Kabul River. Like baby Moses.

LAILA: *(passing back with a bottle of milk)* Her name is Aziza, Aziza, not "that thing." Maybe if we had some proper clothes, you would remember who she is.

RASHEED: What's wrong with her clothes?

LAILA: They are for a boy.

RASHEED: You think she knows the difference? I paid good money for those clothes.

Laila exits.

Can't you do something to help?

MARIAM: What do I know about babies?

RASHEED: That thing is a warlord, I'm telling you, Laila has given birth to a warlord.

Laila enters with the baby in her arms, still crying. Rasheed goes toward her, gentle now or trying to be.

Let Mariam take her for a while, come to bed.

LAILA: I can't, she isn't feeding, maybe this milk is off.

RASHEED: The milk is fine . . . maybe she isn't hungry . . . *(frustrated)* I want you to lay with me now . . .

LAILA: *(quietly, not wanting Mariam to hear)* The doctor said to wait . . .

RASHEED: For one month, she said; it's been twice that, enough is enough. Put the child down.

LAILA: *(pulling away)* How can I? She could be sick, or cold, or she could have a little pain . . .

RASHEED: *(offended at her rebuttal, his gentleness giving way to frustration)* You know, maybe you shouldn't get so attached.

LAILA: *(shocked)* What does that mean?

RASHEED: I was listening to the radio the other night and they said one in four children in Afghanistan will die before the age of five . . . *(Laila glares at him and then storms off. To Mariam)* What's the matter with her?

MARIAM: Her baby is in her arms and you are talking to her about children dying?

RASHEED: I was only telling her what they said . . . *(Mariam shakes her head, smiling.)* What are you smiling at? You think this is funny? You're probably the one egging her on . . . *(He is getting more and more outraged.)* Spending all day and night with that thing wrapped around her, talking back to me, complaining about this and that . . . this is too much for any man to bear . . . this is my house . . . my house . . .

Rasheed follows Laila into the room; he knows she is furious with him. In the kitchen Mariam goes to the window, opens it, leans toward the cool air.

Laila, be reasonable, it's been months, a man has needs.

LAILA: It's too soon, you heard what the doctor said.

RASHEED: *(losing his temper)* Enough about the doctor, it's been months now, put the baby down.

LAILA: No.

RASHEED: *(furious she has defied him but unsure what to do)* I won't tolerate you denying me. I said put the baby down now.

LAILA: *(stares at him defiant)* And I said no!

Rasheed throws something from the bed against the wall; it falls with a bang, making Mariam jump in the other room. He grabs a belt and thunders out.

RASHEED: It's your doing! I know it is.

MARIAM: What are you talking about?

RASHEED: Her denying me, pushing me away, you're teaching her to, well, I won't have it . . . Do you hear me? I won't have it. *(He swings the belt threateningly.)*

Laila comes to the door, Aziza in her arms.

LAILA: Stop it, Rasheed, this has nothing to do with her.

RASHEED: Go back to the room now.

MARIAM: I've said nothing to the girl, I swear . . . *(To Laila)* Tell him.

RASHEED: Shut up . . . you I would expect this from . . . you're bitter and jealous and you want to ruin this for me . . . but I'm telling you now, you leave her alone. She is pure . . . a good girl . . . and here you are corrupting her . . . plotting against me. *(He lunges for Mariam and Laila screams.)*

LAILA: *(pushing herself between him and Mariam, one hand on his arm)* Stop, stop. You win. Don't do this. Please, Rasheed, don't hurt her. You win . . . you win . . .

RASHEED: *(pauses, tries to calm himself, disappointed almost that he had to lose his temper, quietly now to Mariam)* I am on to you, I won't be made a fool of in my own house . . . *(He storms out of the room.)*

Laila walks toward Mariam; they are both shaken. Laila holds out Aziza for Mariam to take.

RASHEED: *(from offstage)* Now, Laila . . .

LAILA: *(to Mariam, pleading)* Please . . .

Mariam takes Aziza, and Laila exits. Mariam stares at Aziza, uncomfortable; she doesn't know what to do with her. She puts her in her basket, but Aziza starts to cry.

MARIAM: Shhh . . . shhh . . . don't you start, we've had enough of shouting for one night . . . *(Aziza giggles and gurgles.)* That's better . . . *(She puts her down again and Aziza cries.)* Okay, shhh, shhh . . . I've got you . . . and what a sorry sight you are, dressed up like a boy and all bundled up in this heat. No wonder you are still awake . . . *(Mariam removes some of the blankets.)* See, that's better, *ney?* *(Aziza gurgles.)* What is it you want? *(She offers her little finger.)* What are you so happy about? You have a brute for a father and a fool for a mother. You wouldn't smile so much if you knew . . . no, you wouldn't . . .

now go to sleep, go on . . . *(Outside the mockingbirds begin to sing.)* You hear that? That's a nightingale . . . you hear it singing? Maybe it is singing for you, little baby, what do you think of that? Eh?

Aziza reaches her hand toward Mariam's face. In this moment Mariam is changed, devoted. She holds the tiny hand to her face and closes her eyes. We move to the other room where Rasheed is leaning back now, smoking, watching Laila, shaking, dress herself.

RASHEED: So what exactly went on between you and that boy Tariq?

LAILA: He was my friend, since childhood, you know that.

RASHEED: I don't know what I know . . . I know the way you used to look at him . . . all the time laughing and smiling. *(Laila says nothing. Rasheed continues to watch her.)* So as friends did you ever . . . do anything out of order?

LAILA: Out of order?

RASHEED: Did he ever, say . . . give you a kiss . . . put his hand where it didn't belong?

LAILA: He was like a brother to me.

RASHEED: Well, which was it? A friend or a brother?

LAILA: Both.

RASHEED: But brothers and sisters are creatures of curiosity. Yes. Sometimes a brother lets his sister see his cock—

LAILA: Don't be disgusting, Rasheed.

RASHEED: I remember people talking, gossiping. They said all sorts of things about you two . . . but if you are saying there was nothing?

LAILA: I am . . .

RASHEED: Then of course I believe you . . . still, though . . . I can't be blamed. I am a husband and these are the things a husband wonders. *(Laila reaches to pull her scarf from the bed. Rasheed purposefully holds on to the end of it.)* I'll tell you one thing . . . he is lucky he died the way he did, because if he were here now and I got my hands on him . . . *(He shakes his head.)*

LAILA: Have you no respect for the dead?

RASHEED: I guess some people can't be dead enough . . .

Laila turns and exits. Pauses in a neutral space. Her grief for Tariq is suddenly very real again. A dream/memory begins as Tariq enters, older now with swagger, smoking a cigarette. Nearby the sound of a party, people talking, etc. 1992.

TARIQ: You found me . . .

LAILA: Your mother would kill you if she knew you were smoking.

TARIQ: Who's gonna tell her? You?

LAILA: Give me one.

TARIQ: No, it's bad for you.

LAILA: And not for you?

TARIQ: I only do it for the girls, they think it's sexy.

LAILA: Are they blind?

TARIQ: You don't think it's sexy?

LAILA: You look like an idiot.

TARIQ: Ouch.

LAILA: What girls anyway?

TARIQ: Why? Are you jealous?

LAILA: No!

TARIQ: *(smiles)* I bet your mother's guests are talking about us now. They are saying that we are canoeing down the river of sin . . .

LAILA: *(giggles)* Riding the rickshaw of wickedness . . .

TARIQ: *(laughs, looks at her)* Your hair is getting longer, it's nice.

LAILA: You changed the subject.

TARIQ: From what?

LAILA: From empty-headed girls who think you're sexy.

TARIQ: You know . . .

LAILA: Know what?

TARIQ: That I only have eyes for you . . .

Laila goes toward him, but he vanishes and the memory fades. She puts her hand on her stomach and waits for the waves of grief to pass.

Lights up in Mariam's room, where she is curled around Aziza, watching her sleep adoringly. Laila enters, still shaken, Mariam sees her and jumps.

LAILA: I didn't mean to startle you. I'll take her—

MARIAM: *(reluctant for Aziza to go)* You can leave her . . . she's sleeping.

An awkward beat. Mariam sits, wants to say something, but doesn't know how to find the words.

What you did tonight . . . no one has ever stood up for me before . . . ever.

LAILA: I couldn't let him beat you, I wasn't raised in a house where people did things like that.

MARIAM: Well, this is your house now, so you better get used to it.

LAILA: I could never get used to violence.

MARIAM: This is the way men are, the same way a dog will bite . . .

LAILA: No . . . not all men . . .

MARIAM: *(looks at her, annoyed almost)* It is the way our husband is . . . and if you're not careful he will turn on you too . . . and you gave him a daughter, so your sin is even worse than mine . . .

LAILA: Than yours?

Mariam looks at her, goes to her wardrobe, takes out a little pile of baby girl's clothes. She hands them to Laila, who looks at them.

For Aziza? They're lovely . . . thank you.

MARIAM: I have no use for them, it is either your daughter or the moths.

LAILA: Did you make them yourself?

MARIAM: I did.

LAILA: When?

MARIAM: *(moves to the window)* When I was pregnant the first time, or maybe the second.

LAILA: *(beat, not sure whether to ask or not)* How many pregnancies were there?

MARIAM: Five, maybe six, I lost count. No one's fault, Allah's will . . . apparently. *(Beat. The two women look at each other, Mariam self-conscious now.)* It was a long time ago, when I first came here, after my mother died . . .

LAILA: Is what Rasheed said true? She hanged herself?

MARIAM: *(quietly, with guilt)* It wasn't her fault . . . it was mine.

LAILA: How could it be yours?

MARIAM: She warned me, but I didn't listen . . . all I wanted was to go to school . . .

Lighting change. Laila stays in the room while Mariam stands and becomes Young Mariam. She lifts a Pinocchio puppet and carries it downstage. Early morning. The kolba. *Spotlight comes up on Mariam as she does her* namaz *prayers. As she finishes we are aware of Mullah Faizullah, a benevolent man in his fifties, sitting behind her, nodding encouragingly. 1974.*

YOUNG MARIAM: More, I want to learn more.

MULLAH FAIZULLAH: I have nothing else to teach you, you know your *namaz* prayers, you can read the Koran.

YOUNG MARIAM: But I don't understand it.

MULLAH FAIZULLAH: No matter, that will come, and in the meantime the prayers will comfort you, you can summon them in your time of need, they will never fail you.

YOUNG MARIAM: But there must be more to learn. My sisters go to the Mehri School for girls in Herat, I want to go too, I want to sit in a classroom and have a teacher. I want to learn every-thing . . . about everything . . .

Nana enters carrying a pail of water in each hand. She's a hardened and bitter woman, a workhorse.

NANA: Did you feed the chickens?

YOUNG MARIAM: Yes, Nana.

NANA: And clean out the coop?

YOUNG MARIAM: Yes, Nana. *(Mariam looks at Mullah Faizullah.)*

MULLAH FAIZULLAH: Mariam tells me she would like to go to school.

NANA: What for?

MULLAH FAIZULLAH: To learn.

NANA: What would be the point? It would be like shining a spit-toon; there is only one skill women like us need, Mariam, and they don't teach it in schools.

Look at me, Mariam. Only one skill you need, and it's this: *tahamul*. Endure.

YOUNG MARIAM: Endure what, Nana?

NANA: Oh, don't you fret about that, there won't be any shortage of things.

She walks into the house.

MULLAH FAIZULLAH: I'm sorry, child.

Mullah Faizullah exits.

YOUNG MARIAM: But what about what I want? Doesn't that matter?

Jalil enters behind her. He's a wealthy man, charming but he lacks conviction. His tie is loosened, his shirt unbuttoned, his jacket slung over his arm.

JALIL: *(arms outstretched)* Where is my little flower?

Young Mariam turns; her face lights up to see him.

YOUNG MARIAM: You came. *(Mariam runs to him and jumps into his arms.)*

JALIL: Of course I came. How could I stay away? Now tell me everything, what have you been doing?

YOUNG MARIAM: Minding the chickens, helping Nana with the meals, I made *sabzi* today.

JALIL: *Sabzi!* Amazing.

YOUNG MARIAM: And I know what I want for my birthday.

JALIL: Anything, tell me.

YOUNG MARIAM: I want you to take me to your cinema. I want to see the real Pinocchio.

JALIL: *(squirms in his seat, coughs)* You know, the picture quality isn't that good, or the sound, the image jumps and sticks; the puppet I brought you is much better than the film. Think of something else.

YOUNG MARIAM: But this is what I want.

JALIL: Well, I work every day, you know, but maybe I can send someone else to take you.

YOUNG MARIAM: *Ney.* I want you to take me. And I want you to invite my brothers and sisters too. I want us to all go together. It's what I want . . . please . . .

JALIL: *(stares at her, pained)* Come here. *(He pulls her into an embrace and holds her there.)* Tomorrow at noon. I'll meet you by the river.

YOUNG MARIAM: Thank you . . . *(Jalil leaves; she stares after him, delighted.)* Tomorrow . . . tomorrow . . . tomorrow . . .

Passage of time. Mariam wraps a pretty scarf about her in anticipation. Laila watches. Mariam waits and waits; the sun begins to drop from the sky. Nana walks forward, bucket in each hand.

NANA: Did you really think he would come? Bring you into the town as one of his own? *(Mariam stands.)* Remember, he betrayed us. *(Mariam ignores her.)* You know what he told his wives when I started to show? That I forced myself on him. Me? A servant in his house? *(She shakes her head at the thought of it.)* Then he cast us out to live up here in a hut out of sight. Don't you see? This is what it means to be a woman in this world. Look at me. *(She lifts Mariam's chin with her finger.)* Like a compass needle that points north, a man's accusing finger always finds a woman. Always. *(Mariam shakes her off, starts to walk away from the* kolba.*)* Where are you going? People will point at you and stare, they will throw rocks, call you a *harami,* they will chase you from the town . . . *(Mariam continues to walk. Nana flies after her now, grabs her desperately.)*

How dare you abandon me after all I have endured for you? *(Mariam goes and Nana grabs her, wraps her arms around her, her face pressed to her stomach. She looks up at Mariam.)* Don't go. You know I love you, Mariam jo? I can't lose you to him . . . I'll die if you go . . . I'll die . . .

Laila comes forward, cutting the memory of Nana off.

LAILA: How could she say those things to you? You were only a child—

MARIAM: But she was right, she was right about him, all along. She warned me that he would betray me the way he had betrayed her.

LAILA: And did he?

MARIAM: Oh, yes . . . even after I walked for miles to get to his house, he didn't even let me in. He sent his driver to turn me away . . .

She sits on the ground, becoming Young Mariam outside Jalil's gates. The Driver appears.

DRIVER: What, still here? I told you last night he is not home. You've made a scene, it's time to go.

YOUNG MARIAM: I'm waiting for my father.

DRIVER: Listen to me, Mr. Khan has told me I am to take you home. Do you understand? He told me.

YOUNG MARIAM: *(pushes past him)* There, I saw him, at the window, I saw him . . . he's been there all night? He left me to sleep outside on the ground like a dog all night?

DRIVER: Come on now . . . that is enough . . . I'm taking you home to your mother.

The Driver leads Mariam upstage toward the kolba. *Lights up suddenly on the silhouette of Nana's body, hanging from a tree by her neck. Mariam screams. She barely has time to absorb the image before Jalil enters, guilty. He can't look her in the eye. Mariam is in shock.*

JALIL: I'm so sorry about your mother . . . it's very sad . . . but I have good news. You have a suitor.

YOUNG MARIAM: A what?

JALIL: A *khastegar,* a suitor, his name is Rasheed. A Pashtun, he lives in Kabul. He's a shoemaker, he has his own shop, he can provide for you.

YOUNG MARIAM: *(to Jalil)* Why can't I stay here with you?

JALIL: *(pained, looks down)* He is a little older than you.

YOUNG MARIAM: *(desperate now)* I don't want this. Don't make me.

JALIL: *(struggling to meet her gaze)* I have already given my answer . . .

Rasheed enters with Mariam's suitcase. He shakes Jalil's hand.

RASHEED: Let's go, my dear. *(Mariam stares at Jalil; heartbroken, she turns to go.)*

JALIL: Mariam, wait.

YOUNG MARIAM: I used to worship you, I prayed you would live to be a hundred years old, I didn't know you were ashamed of me.

JALIL: I'll visit you.

YOUNG MARIAM: No. It ends here for you and me. Don't come. I won't see you. I don't ever want to hear from you again.

Rasheed exits as Laila comes forward.

LAILA: You must have hated him for giving you away . . .

MARIAM: *(beat; thinks; time has dulled this pain somewhat)* I did hate him, but I hated myself more, for what I had done to my mother . . . and even when I thought I had found my own happiness . . . she never let me go . . . *(The ghost of Nana appears.)*

NANA: You think this is a blessing?

YOUNG MARIAM: *(picks up one of the items of baby clothes from the pile and stares at it in delight)* I'm going to be a mother, Nana. *(She pauses, laughs.)* A mother. Me. The doctor said it was no bigger than a fingernail, just a tiny thing but with a heart beating already, beating fast. I thought I could hear it all the

way home on the bus, and everywhere I looked the city seemed
to me to be singing . . .

NANA: It will break your heart, that's all children can do . . .

YOUNG MARIAM: Let me be, Nana, let me be happy . . .

*Nana withdraws. Young Mariam turns away and puts her hands on
her stomach. Then she suddenly pitches forward in pain, lifts her hands
to find blood. It stains the baby clothes in her hands; she panics. Rasheed enters, furious and heartbroken.*

RASHEED: We paid the doctor his fee, we want a better answer
than that . . . God's will . . .

YOUNG MARIAM: *(crushed)* Maybe we should have a burial . . . or
say a few prayers at least—

RASHEED: What's the point?

YOUNG MARIAM: To mark it, to say good-bye . . .

RASHEED: Then you do it, I've already buried one son, I won't
bury another . . .

*Rasheed exits. Mariam keels over, the grief winding her. She calls out
for her mother.*

YOUNG MARIAM: Nana . . . Nana . . . Nana . . .

*Nana comes to her, takes the bloodied baby clothes from her, cradles
them in her arms.*

NANA: *Tahamul.* Endure . . .

*Nana walks back into the darkness, leaving Mariam alone and heart-
broken. Laila watches her, overwhelmed by what she has heard. Laila*

takes hold of Mariam's hand. Mariam looks at it oddly, like a bird that has landed on her.

LAILA: *(holds her hand still)* All that has happened to you . . .

MARIAM: *(stares at Laila, softens)* Well . . . we have all had our own tragedies . . .

LAILA: None of this was your fault.

Mariam nods, moved, releases her hand. They sit in this strange new space for a beat, neither wanting to break it.

I could make us some tea . . . We could have it outside. Rasheed won't wake for hours yet. *(Mariam looks at her. Beat. Knows this is an olive branch but not sure how to respond.)* There is some *halwa* left over . . . *Halwa* is awfully good with tea.

Mariam absorbs this, doesn't know how to take it, a wave of emotion building within her.

LAILA: Just one cup . . .

MARIAM: *(beat)* Yes . . . yes.

The two women look at each other. The war is over. In the transition into the next scene they begin to work together to complete the chores, a synchronicity to their movements, an ease finally between them.

SCENE SIX

Sounds of gunfire in the distance, men shouting. Rasheed begins hammering wooden planks across the front door. His head is bleeding; he mops at it with a bloody handkerchief between hammering. He is in a foul humor. Laila and Mariam enter with a crying Aziza. 1994.

LAILA: What's all this? *(goes to look at his head)* What happened to your head? Were you attacked?

Aziza wails even louder.

RASHEED: Would you shut her up?

Rasheed exits. Aziza whimpers as Rasheed storms out. Mariam takes her in her arms. Laila watches her with Aziza.

LAILA: She adores you.

MARIAM: Don't mind him, he's a brute, I told you.

LAILA: Sometimes I think about putting chili in his toothpaste; you think Allah would forgive me?

MARIAM: I know I would . . .

Laila and Mariam laugh as Rasheed enters, sees them, paranoid.

RASHEED: Where's my meal? I said where is it? What have you been doing all day, huh? Talking and sniggering? Is it too much to expect food to be ready when I come home from work? *(He continues to hammer planks across the doorway.)*

LAILA: But how are we to get out?

RASHEED: I told you what I have seen out there. Dostum and Hekmatyar's men are firing on Massoud and Rabbani forces from either side of the Kabul River. Regular people are being killed daily, by the dozen, unprovoked. Yesterday the hospital was shelled, they aren't letting emergency food vehicles into the city, it's a war zone out there, and I am the only one protecting you from it.

LAILA: But Aziza needs milk.

RASHEED: *(through gritted teeth)* She will have to do without . . .

He looks at the boarded-up door, mops at his bloody head. Takes a gun from inside his jacket and examines it. Mariam and Laila are shocked.

MARIAM: Where did you get that?

RASHEED: What do you think will stop us being killed in our beds? You think they can be talked out of it? You're so stupid . . . so ignorant . . .

Mariam puts a plate before him. Rasheed scowls, tastes it, makes a fuss about spitting it out.

This rice is overcooked.

MARIAM: I took it off the heat in plenty of time.

RASHEED: And the meat is tough and greasy. Can you not get even the simplest thing right? Could your crazy mother not even teach you that much?

Mariam is stung by this; she turns away. Laila goes to stand near her, watches Rasheed, angry.

LAILA: What happened to your head, Rasheed? Did someone beat you up?

Rasheed looks at her dangerously.

RASHEED: You have any idea what I risk just to put food on your plate? *(He looks away, furious.)* There are looters everywhere . . . *(He turns to Laila.)* They barged into my shop, took everything that they could, and destroyed the rest . . . just for the sake of it . . . just because they could . . . *(He looks up at Laila.)* Do you know what that means? No shop . . . no money . . .

LAILA: *(worried)* Did you report it?

RASHEED: *(sneering)* Report it? To whom? Do you know who is in charge out there? The same men your stupid brothers gave their lives to fight for, the same ones your mother prayed would oust the Soviets . . . they are nothing but dogs! You see how stupid your brothers were? You see what kind of men they put on a pedestal?

LAILA: Don't you speak of my family—

This is too close to the bone. Rasheed slams his hand on the table.

RASHEED: Shut your mouth! Do you hear me? You want to know what the Mujahideen's men are doing to women? Beating, raping . . . yes . . . rape . . . they pluck women off the street and give them to their militiamen as rewards . . . and afterward their own fathers and husbands kill them for the shame of it . . . You see how lucky you are? To be protected by me?

LAILA: *(refuses to give him the respect he wants, sarcastic)* Oh, yes . . . we're very lucky . . .

Mariam can't help it; she smiles at Laila's sarcasm.

RASHEED: You think it's funny? What I'm saying? You think it's a joke?

MARIAM: No . . .

In a second Rasheed is on top of Mariam. He grabs her, pulls her back to the table, and pushes her face into the plate of food roughly. She struggles.

LAILA: Leave her be.

RASHEED: Let her eat it, if she thinks it's worth eating.

LAILA: She can't breathe.

RASHEED: So? Since when do you care if she breathes or not? I see the two of you every day now, heads together, talking, laughing, what are you laughing at? Huh? Me? You think I don't know that? You think I'm stupid?

LAILA: Let her go . . . please . . .

Rasheed waits a beat and then lets go of Mariam; she falls backward, gasping for air, wiping food from her face.

RASHEED: So what was so funny?

MARIAM: *(shakes her head)* Nothing . . .

Another incoming shell is heard. Rasheed listens, frightened and hating it. Aziza begins to wail.

RASHEED: And you, stop whining, be quiet, can't you . . . *(Aziza continues to cry. Rasheed points the gun at her in anger.)* I said shut up!

Mariam and Laila freeze, not sure what Rasheed will do next. Terrified, Laila moves slowly to where she lies and picks her up. Rasheed is now pointing the gun at her.

You know, it's an interesting eye color she has, neither yours nor mine. *(Laila freezes; Aziza wails again.)* I'm warning you. You shut her up.

He realizes he is out of control. He exits suddenly. Mariam and Laila are shaken. Laila sits down, holds Aziza tightly to her. Another shell lands. Mariam comes to them, wraps her arms around both of them. Another explosion takes us out of this scene and into the next one.

SCENE SEVEN

Night. The house is quiet except for the singing of a nightingale. Rasheed lies sleeping in his room. Laila creeps from their bed and goes to Mariam's room, where she is pacing anxiously.

LAILA: Don't make a sound . . .

MARIAM: *(turns and sees her, worried)* Aziza?

LAILA: She's fine . . . listen . . . *(Beat.)* Aziza and I . . . we're leaving.

MARIAM: *(confused)* Leaving where?

LAILA: Here . . . I've been stealing from him, just a little at a time, I've hidden the money in the lining of my dress. I have a thousand afghani, that's enough for the bus fare to Peshawar and to keep us going for a while when we get there.

MARIAM: When?

LAILA: Now, before he wakes.

MARIAM: It's not possible.

LAILA: But it is, we can change things, we just have to try . . . come with us . . .

MARIAM: How can I?

LAILA: How can you not? How can you stay here if leaving is an option?

MARIAM: But it isn't . . . it won't work. Women are forbidden to travel without a male relative, you know what they will do if they catch us?

LAILA: We'll find someone at the station, I'll say I'm a widow, someone will take pity on us.

MARIAM: And if we get to Pakistan? Rasheed said two million Afghan refugees have already fled there, the borders are closed, we have no visas—it won't work.

LAILA: We will make it work, we will find a way to make it work. What choice do we have? How long before he kills one of us? Maybe even Aziza? *(A noise from offstage makes them both look up in fear.)* She's the reason we can't stay here . . . *(She sits closer now, aware of the danger of this secret.)* The night before Tariq left he came to me . . .

Tariq enters, another memory coming back to life. 1992.

TARIQ: I'm saying we're leaving.

LAILA: No.

TARIQ: Tomorrow . . . we're going to Peshawar first, then I don't know after. Maybe Hindustan or Iran . . . I was going to tell you, Laila, I swear . . . It's my father. His heart can't take it anymore, all this fighting and killing and my mother is so afraid all the time. Laila . . . please look at me . . . *(Beat.)* I want to marry you, today, and then you can come with me.

LAILA: I told him I couldn't . . .

TARIQ: We'll go to a mosque, find a mullah—

LAILA: But I should have said yes . . . yes . . .

TARIQ: Your father will give his blessing, I know he will.

Babi appears suddenly. Laila goes to him. 1992.

BABI: I'm so glad I have you, Laila. Every day I thank God for you. Every single day. Sometimes when your mother is having one of her really dark days, I feel like you are all I have . . .

LAILA: How could I leave my father? How could I?

Babi fades into the darkness. Tariq comes to her now.

TARIQ: *(devastated)* But I love you . . . *(He reaches out to her, kisses her.)* I love you . . . *(She responds; it's a hungry and desperate embrace.)* I love you . . . *(Tariq disappears as the memory fades. Laila turns back to Mariam.)*

LAILA: I thought I might never see him again and I loved him so much . . . and what we did we did out of love . . . *(Mariam is not getting it.)* Aziza . . . is our love made flesh. *(Mariam is in shock; she stares from Aziza to Laila and back again.)* And Rasheed already suspects, I know he does; what if one day he makes up his mind? What will he do to her? Give her away? Shoot her? How can I sit here and wait for that to happen? We have to go. *(Mariam is in shock.)* Mariam . . .

Mariam backs away, shaking her head; she cannot process this.

LAILA: He will wake soon . . . we have to go now . . .

Mariam still struggling, shell-shocked. She looks away from Laila, trying to find the answer within herself.

MARIAM: And why shouldn't I?

From the darkness Nana walks toward her. Mariam looks from her to Laila, frantically trying to choose.

How could I stay here without them? How could I?

Nana withdraws, rejected. Mariam takes strength from being able to banish her. A noise from offstage.

LAILA: *(terrified, desperate)* Mariam!

Mariam looks at her, their whole future hanging in the balance. Lights down.

Act Two

SCENE ONE

The noise and sounds of Lahore station come to life before us. Lights up to reveal Mariam and Laila huddled together, Aziza in Mariam's arms. The noise and bustle of the station seem to intimidate them. 1994.

LAILA: Do you see anyone?

MARIAM: I am looking . . .

LAILA: *(nodding covertly)* What about him?

MARIAM: No.

LAILA: Why not?

MARIAM: He looks too mean.

LAILA: *(nodding to another)* Him?

MARIAM: Too old . . . him?

LAILA: Too fat.

MARIAM: *(admonishing)* Laila . . .

LAILA: Look there . . .

Mariam looks as Wakil, a young man, enters with his wife cradling a baby in her arms; Laila and Mariam eye him up.

He is young and he looks kind, don't you think?

MARIAM: I can't tell . . .

LAILA: Wait here.

MARIAM: Be careful.

Laila approaches Wakil.

LAILA: Forgive me, brother, but are you going to Peshawar?

WAKIL: Yes.

LAILA: I wonder if you might help us?

WAKIL: What is it, *hamshira*?

LAILA: I am a *biwa*, my husband was killed by a shell. I'm here with my mother and my daughter and we have no one left in Kabul. I have an uncle in Peshawar, he has promised to take us in and—

WAKIL: And you want to travel with my family?

LAILA: I know it's *zahmat* for you . . . but you look kind, brother, and I hoped you might understand.

WAKIL: Don't worry, *hamshira*, I understand, it's no trouble. Why don't I go and buy your tickets?

LAILA: Oh, thank you, brother, thank you. *(She fishes in her burqa and produces an envelope of money; she hands it to him.)* This is a good deed, brother, God will remember it.

WAKIL: *(takes the envelope)* Wait there . . .

Wakil walks away; his wife and child go with him. Laila smiles at the woman, then returns to Mariam.

MARIAM: What did he say?

LAILA: He is buying the tickets.

MARIAM: Are you sure?

LAILA: He has kind eyes, Mariam, he will come back, I know it . . . *(They both stare after Wakil, waiting.)* I'm so nervous, I feel sick.

MARIAM: I know, me too.

LAILA: How long has it been now?

MARIAM: Five minutes . . .

LAILA: And now?

MARIAM: Ten minutes . . .

LAILA: He will come . . . *(Beat.)* And now?

MARIAM: Half an hour . . . *(worried)* Laila . . .

LAILA: Have faith, Mariam.

Another long beat, then finally Wakil appears with his wife and child. Laila and Mariam almost melt with relief.

WAKIL: Time to go. I'll hold on to your tickets, it will look better. What is your name?

LAILA: I am Laila, this is my mother, Mariam, and my daughter, Aziza.

WAKIL: My name is Wakil and if they ask, then say you are my cousin . . . stay close and we will all board together.

A line begins to form to get on the bus. Laila and Mariam are giddy with relief.

LAILA: Thank you.

MARIAM: For what?

LAILA: For coming with us, I don't think I could do this alone.

MARIAM: You don't have to . . .

A Militiaman is checking tickets. When it is Wakil's turn, he hands them his tickets, then leans in and says something to the Militiaman. He looks at Laila and Mariam.

MILITIAMAN: You two, step aside.

Mariam and Laila panic, do nothing.

   I said step aside . . .

LAILA: What's the problem, brother?

MILITIAMAN: Hurry up, you're holding up the line.

LAILA: But we have tickets, didn't my cousin give them to you?

MILITIAMAN: *(grabs Laila roughly by the arm)* Stop talking . . .

(He starts to drag her away from the bus, Mariam and Aziza following.)

LAILA: We have tickets, I'm telling you, we have to get on the bus, we have tickets, why are you doing this?

The Militiaman drags her into an interview room. Lights snap up on the Interrogator in a dark suit sitting patiently as Laila is thrown onto the chair opposite. He speaks quietly, cleaning his glasses, reserved, as if he believes he is somehow above all this. The Militiaman stands to attention behind Laila for the duration.

INTERROGATOR: We know that you have already told one lie today, *hamshira*. The man at the station was not your cousin, he told us so himself, so the question now is if you will tell us more lies. Personally, I would advise against it . . .

LAILA: I'm telling you the truth, we were going to stay with my uncle.

INTERROGATOR: The woman out there in the corridor, she's your mother?

LAILA: Yes.

INTERROGATOR: Interesting . . . and you say you are widowed . . . my condolences . . . and this uncle of yours . . . what is his name? Surely you remember his name, *hamshira*?

LAILA: I do. Of course. Mr. Ali, Reza Ali.

INTERROGATOR: And where does he live?

LAILA: In Peshawar.

INTERROGATOR: Interesting . . . where in Peshawar? *(Laila stares at him blankly.)* What neighborhood? Which street? What sector number?

LAILA: Jamrud Road.

INTERROGATOR: Oh, yes, the same street as the Pearl Continental Hotel, maybe he mentioned it to you?

LAILA: Yes, that's right, the very same street . . .

INTERROGATOR: Except that the Pearl Continental Hotel isn't on Jamrud Road . . .

Laila panics. Pauses, trying to think. We hear the sound of Aziza crying in the distance.

LAILA: That's my daughter crying, she's frightened, may I go to her, brother?

INTERROGATOR: I prefer "officer." You do realize that running away is a crime? That the punishment is imprisonment?

LAILA: *(knows her lies are futile, changes tack)* Please, Officer . . . let us go . . . what does it matter to you to let two women go? What's the harm in it? We are not criminals.

INTERROGATOR: It's the law. Women don't seem to realize how dangerous it is for them in these times of turmoil. A woman traveling alone is not safe. It's our responsibility to protect you.

LAILA: If you send us back, he will kill us, what about your responsibility then?

INTERROGATOR: What a man does in his own home is his own business.

LAILA: Even if that means killing his wife?

INTERROGATOR: *(standing)* This interview is over . . . I must say you have made a very poor case for yourself . . . very poor indeed . . . take her out.

The Militiaman grabs both Laila and Mariam and pushes them across the stage. Lights up on Rasheed, standing lit from behind, an ominous shadow in silhouette. He steps forward. His face contorted, he is angry, yes, but there is more to it. He is also heartbroken in a way, betrayed.

RASHEED: What were you thinking? *(Beat. The two women are frozen with fear.)* Were you thinking at all? Do you have any idea what could have happened to you? To all of you? The kind of people who are out there? *(Beat.)* I expected more from both of you . . . especially you, Laila . . . *(In his voice, there is heartbreak.)* Especially you . . . *(Beat.)* So what would you have me do now? What is the correct response to the shame and indignity you have brought upon my house? *(He goes to Laila, getting angry now.)* Say something . . . defend yourself . . . defend your actions . . . *(Laila cannot speak. His anger is growing.)* It is my responsibility to protect my family and that is what I will do . . . make sure you never do this again . . . do you understand? *(Laila does not respond.)* Take the child to the bedroom . . . *(Laila goes to pull Mariam with her.)* No . . . Mariam stays here . . . *(Laila doesn't move. Rasheed is shouting now.)* Go!

Laila walks off, looking back at Mariam. Rasheed takes a step toward her, lights down.

SCENE TWO

Lights up. Laila and Aziza huddled on the bed in their room. Laila singing softly to Aziza. We hear Mariam scream, the dull thump, thump, thump of a beating follows. Laila rocks Aziza in her arms.

LAILA: Hush now, baby, everything will be all right, everything will be all right . . .

The passage of time, a sun crossing the sky, the morning prayers ringing out, a day has passed. Scorching heat. Laila weak now, Aziza lying with her head on her lap. Another scream from Mariam. Laila, driven mad by the sound of Mariam's beating.

Mariam jan . . . Mariam jan . . .

Lights up on Rasheed beating Mariam in slow exaggerated movements. Mariam steps away, shrugs from her burqa, but Rasheed continues to hit the burqa. Mariam watches on as Nana steps from the shadows.

MARIAM: *(beat)* Will he kill me?

NANA: It's possible, where there are men involved it is always possible.

MARIAM: At least he is not beating them.

NANA: No . . . he's starving them instead . . .

Mariam looks toward where Laila and Aziza are. Another day has passed. Now Laila is wild, dehydrated, Aziza a limp creature in her arms.

LAILA: *(whispering)* Soon, little one, soon . . . we'll have milk soon . . . you just be patient . . . be a good patient little girl and Mammy will get you some milk . . . Aziza? *(Laila claws at the door weakly.)* Rasheed? Please . . . please, just some milk, Rasheed . . . not for me, for her . . . she is innocent in all this . . . do it for her . . . you don't want her blood on your hands . . . please . . . *(No response. She returns to Aziza, begins to shake her gently.)*

Aziza? Don't leave me, my darling, stay, stay, and I'll tell you all about your father, your baba, your real baba, so kind and gentle . . . Aziza?

The passage of time again, another sunset and sunrise. Mariam is now back in her burqa, lying bent and broken, her head resting on Nana's lap.

NANA: Not far now . . . almost there . . . I am waiting . . . I am waiting . . .

Laila and Aziza are unconscious now. The sound of a door being unlocked and Rasheed is there, panting from the exertion of beating Mariam, anxious, not in control. He goes down on his haunches, almost wants to touch her. Laila raises her head weakly.

LAILA: *(weakly)* Mariam?

RASHEED: I told you it would be Mariam who would pay for your misbehavior . . . I told you . . . *(Beat.)* All I want is to look after you, why won't you let me? *(He reaches out to touch her face. She pulls away, the revulsion she feels for him clear in her expression. Rasheed sees it too for the first time, sees that she hates him. An eerie hardness comes through him now.)* So this is how you want it to be? *(Beat. There is no answer from Laila.)* Fine . . . know this . . . if you try this again I will find you. I swear on the Prophet's name that I will find you. And when I do, there isn't a court in this godforsaken country that will hold me accountable for what I will do. To Mariam first, then to her, then you last. I will make you watch. You understand me? I'll make you watch.

Laila struggles to stand. Lights down.

In the transition, flyers drop from above like snowflakes. Aziza, now eight, picks one up and walks into the next scene.

SCENE THREE

Aziza reads from the flyer. Mariam listens attentively nearby. Laila, pregnant, is kneading bread and listening also. Aziza stumbles over some of the words. She is excited, as if this flyer might bring exciting news.

AZIZA: Our *watan* is now known as the Islamic Emirate of Afghanistan. These are the laws that we will enforce and you will obey: All citizens must pray five times a day, if it is prayer time and you are caught doing something else you will be beaten. All men will grow their beards. All boys will wear turbans. Singing is forbidden. Dancing is forbidden. Playing cards—

LAILA: Cards?

AZIZA: Shhh, Mammy . . . I'm reading . . .

LAILA: Sorry . . .

AZIZA: Playing cards, chess, gambling, and kite flying are forbidden.

LAILA: Kites? This is ridiculous.

AZIZA: Mammy . . . stop interrupting.

MARIAM: Go on, Aziza . . .

AZIZA: Writing books, watching films, and painting pictures are forbidden. If you keep parakeets, you will be beaten and the birds killed.

MARIAM: What did parakeets ever do to the Taliban?

Aziza giggles at this, as does Mariam, a secret smile between them. They adore each other.

LAILA: I see you don't tell your Khala Mariam to stop interrupting.

AZIZA: If you steal, your hand will be cut off at the wrist. If you steal again, your foot will be cut off.

MARIAM: If people are stealing, it is because they are starving.

Over the following Aziza becomes more somber as she reads. Laila and Mariam are more concerned.

AZIZA: Attention, women: You will stay inside your homes at all times. If you go out, you must be accompanied by a male relative. If you are caught alone, you will be beaten and sent home. You will not, under any circumstance, show your face. You will cover with a burqa when outside. Cosmetics are forbidden. Jewelry is forbidden. You will not wear charming clothes. You will not speak unless spoken to. You will not make eye contact with men. You will not laugh in public. You will not paint your nails. If you do, you will lose a finger. Girls are forbidden from attending school. All girls' schools are to be closed immediately. *(Aziza looks at Laila, upset now.)* No school, Mammy? Why?

MARIAM: They can't do that, Aziza has to go to school, she has to . . . this can't be right . . . you read it, Laila.

Laila wipes flour from her hands and takes the flyer herself.

LAILA: Women are forbidden from working. If you are found guilty of adultery, you will be stoned to death. Listen. Listen well. Obey. *Allah-u-akbar* . . .

MARIAM: *(taking this in)* Let's hope that baby in your belly is a boy . . .

LAILA: Why?

MARIAM: Because this country has declared war on women . . .

Rasheed enters. He no longer looks at Laila with adoration but with cynicism, his guard up. Laila turns to him in desperation, the flyer in her hand.

RASHEED: So you've heard. The Taliban have reached Kabul.

LAILA: They can't make half the population stay at home and do nothing.

RASHEED: Why not?

LAILA: This isn't some village. It's Kabul. Women here used to practice law and medicine, they held office in government—

RASHEED: Spoken like the arrogant daughter of a poetry-reading university man that you are. How urbane, how Tajik, of you. *(Mariam leads Aziza offstage, never sure what Rasheed will do next.)* You think this is some new, radical idea that the Taliban

are bringing? Have you ever lived outside of your precious little shell in Kabul? Ever been to visit the real Afghanistan in
the south, the east, along the tribal border with Pakistan? No?
I have. And I can tell you that there are many places in this
country that have always lived this way, or close enough any-
how. Not that you would know.

LAILA: They are savages.

RASHEED: Compared to what? The Soviets killed a million people. The Mujahideen killed fifty thousand in Kabul alone
over the past four years. Fifty thousand. Is it so insensible, in
comparison, to chop the hands off a few thieves? It's in the
Koran, after all, an eye for an eye, tooth for a tooth. If someone killed Aziza, wouldn't you want to avenge her . . . *(Laila
glares at him.)* I'm just making a point . . . *(Rasheed comes closer
to Laila.)* You know, if the fancy should strike me—and I'm
not saying it will—but it could—I would be well within my
rights to give Aziza away. How would you like that? Or I
could go to the Taliban one day, just walk in and say that I
have my suspicions about you. That's all it would take. Whose
word do you think they would believe? What do you think
they would do to you? *(Long beat. Laila tries to force herself not
to look at him, but she can't help herself. He sees the fear in her eyes
and smiles.)* Not that I would. *Ney.* Probably not . . .

LAILA: You're despicable.

RASHEED: *(comes even closer)* That's a big word. I've always dis-
liked that about you. Even when you were little, when you
were running about with that cripple, you thought you were so
clever . . . *(He picks up Babi's book, which is lying somewhere
nearby. Laila watches him, worried.)*

LAILA: Give it to me . . .

RASHEED: What for? What good are books to you now? What's keeping you off the streets, your smarts or me? I'm despicable? Half the women in this city would kill to have a husband like me. They would kill for it . . . you like big words? *(He tucks the book into his jacket.)* I'll give you one. Perspective . . .

Laila doubles over. Rasheed exits, satisfied; when Laila rises again, she lets out an unearthly scream. Mariam comes forward and helps her walk into the hospital waiting room. A line of people has formed around a Doctor wearing a blood-stained white burqa. Perhaps some Talib militiamen with guns pass through this scene; they are everywhere now.

LAILA: I've heard they have no electricity here, no clean water here, no oxygen, no medications . . .

MARIAM: Hush now, I'll get someone who can help.

Mariam pushes to the head of the line.

MARIAM: Doctor, my daughter's water broke, but the baby won't come.

DOCTOR: Does she have a fever?

MARIAM: No.

DOCTOR: Bleeding?

MARIAM: No.

DOCTOR: We will get to her.

MARIAM: When?

DOCTOR: As soon as we can.

The Doctor exits and Mariam returns to Laila.

MARIAM: *(trying to stay calm)* Someone is coming. Everything will be okay . . .

LAILA: Mariam . . .

MARIAM: Yes?

LAILA: You are a terrible liar . . .

Again Laila doubles over in pain; she screams, and when she sits up again, the lights have changed state. We are in the basic operating theater now; a clothesline hangs overhead with surgical gloves pinned to it. The Doctor now stands above her.

DOCTOR: First baby?

MARIAM: Second.

DOCTOR: Any problems with the first delivery?

MARIAM: No.

DOCTOR: Are you her mother?

MARIAM: *(without hesitation)* Yes.

DOCTOR: I have to feel the baby now, *hamshira. (She pulls on the gloves and examines Laila.)* Your daughter needs a cesarean, do you know what that is?

MARIAM: No.

DOCTOR: Her baby is lying in the wrong position, so it isn't able to come out on its own. We will have to open her womb and take the baby out. There is something else . . . *(She lowers her voice.)* We have no anesthetic.

MARIAM: But how will she stand it?

LAILA: What's going on?

DOCTOR: What can we do? We have no oxygen, no suction, no X-ray, we don't even have antibiotics. When the NGOs offer help, the Taliban turn it away or give it to the men's hospitals.

MARIAM: Can I buy the medicine myself?

LAILA: Is the baby okay?

DOCTOR: There is no time . . . this baby needs to come out now.

LAILA: I know . . . *(They turn to look at her.)* I know there is no anesthetic; I don't care, do it, cut me open and give me my baby . . .

A nurse comes forward, erects a makeshift curtain between the Doctor and her. The Doctor removes her burqa.

DOCTOR: They want us to operate in a burqa . . . but I refuse . . . *The Doctor prepares. Mariam comes to stand near Laila's head; she strokes her hair.*

LAILA: One day this will just become another story to tell, the day my baby was born, we will laugh about this, we will drink tea and laugh. Won't we?

MARIAM: *(terrified, trying to stay strong)* Yes . . . yes . . .

DOCTOR: *(looks down at Laila as a nurse hands her a scalpel)* Take heart, little sister, take heart . . .

She bends over Laila, a single moment, a blinding flash of white light, a silent scream frozen on Laila's face . . . like an image from a Caravaggio painting. Then lights down.

In the transition—time passing, seasons changing, Kabul becoming more damaged, more desperate. Zalmai, five, runs across the stage.

SCENE FOUR

Laila and Mariam are folding laundry.

ZALMAI: I want to play . . .

Aziza, now thirteen, enters, wearing a scarf draped around her like a gown. She jumps on Mariam.

AZIZA: I'm Jack!

LAILA: Quiet, Aziza jan!

AZIZA: Jack, say my name, Khala Mariam, say it, Jack!

ZALMAI: Ziza . . .

Talib soldiers cross upstage speaking Farsi.

LAILA: Quiet!

They all wait fearfully for them to pass and exit.

AZIZA: They can't hear us.

LAILA: And what if they do? You know watching movies is forbidden.

AZIZA: *(turns back to Mariam, ignoring Laila)* I'm Jack and you are Rose . . . say it . . . *(She jumps on Mariam, pinning her to the ground.)*

MARIAM: Fine . . . fine . . . you are Jack and I am Rose . . . that's fine . . . you die young and I get to live to a ripe old age . . .

ZALMAI: Who do I get to be?

AZIZA: Yes, but I am a hero . . . while you, Rose, you spend your entire, miserable life longing for me . . . now we must kiss! *(Aziza tries to kiss Mariam while she tries to dodge her, much giggling and hysterics.)*

LAILA: What is it with this movie? It's like the city has gone *Titanic* mad . . . On the black market I've seen *Titanic* carpets, *Titanic* deodorant, *Titanic* perfume, I even saw a woman buying a *Titanic* burqa.

MARIAM: It's the song.

AZIZA: No, it's Leo . . . *(sighing)* it's all about Leo.

LAILA: Ah yes . . . everybody wants Jack, that's what it is. Everybody wants Jack to rescue them from disaster. But there is no Jack. Jack is not coming back. Jack is dead.

AZIZA: No, he's not, he's right here, I am Jack, now kiss me!

ZALMAI: *(shouting now)* Aziza!

AZIZA: *(irritated)* What?

ZALMAI: Who do I get to be?

AZIZA: You can be the iceberg.

ZALMAI: I don't want to be the iceberg, I want to be Jack.

AZIZA: I'm Jack.

ZALMAI: But I want to be Jack, I'm telling Baba.

LAILA: No, Zalmai, don't wake your father.

ZALMAI: *(turns coyly, knows he has the upper hand)* So I can be Jack?

Laila and Aziza exchange a look.

AZIZA: Fine . . . I don't care . . . I don't even want to play anymore anyway . . .

Zalmai runs over and kicks Aziza; she screeches.

MARIAM: Zalmai . . . don't kick your sister.

ZALMAI: Baba says I can do whatever I want.

LAILA: He didn't mean kicking your sister.

ZALMAI: I want my television, Baba bought it for me, I want it.

LAILA: Shhh now, you know we're not allowed to have it, it's buried in the yard.

ZALMAI: But I want it.

LAILA: Shhh, Zalmai . . . please . . .

Rasheed enters, unkempt, hungry, and irritated.

RASHEED: What's all this noise?

LAILA: He's kicking Aziza.

RASHEED: What did you do to annoy him? Eh?

AZIZA: Nothing.

RASHEED: *(takes hold of her ear aggressively)* You leave your brother alone, he can do whatever he wants . . . *(He lets go and Aziza falls back, hurt. Rasheed turns to Zalmai.)* Look what your baba got for you last night. *(Rasheed produces a miniature basketball from inside his coat and gives it to Zalmai.)*

ZALMAI: *(delighted)* A ball! A ball!

RASHEED: *(also takes a small piece of bread from his pocket and gives it to Zalmai)* And some bread. Eat it all now, okay? Good boy.

ZALMAI: Yes, Baba . . .

Mariam, Laila, and Aziza watch Zalmai eat the piece of bread; they are all ravenous. Aziza can't take it; she exits, followed by Mariam.

LAILA: Zalmai, go play in the yard.

Zalmai exits, playing with the ball; Laila watches Rasheed fiddling with his radio.

Is that it?

RASHEED: Is what it?

LAILA: Is that all the food you brought?

RASHEED: *(turns to Laila and looks at her)* What has happened to you anyway? I married a pretty young girl and now I'm sad-dled with a hag . . . Look at you, you are turning into Mariam.

LAILA: *(biting her tongue)* You should go, you'll be late for work at the kebab shop.

RASHEED: I'm not going to work.

LAILA: What?

RASHEED: Monkey-faced Uzbek fired me . . .

LAILA: Well, that's great.

RASHEED: I won't take orders from an idiot like him.

LAILA: And what are we supposed to eat? You owe money to every lender in town.

RASHEED: Shut your mouth.

LAILA: Wasting money on new toys and clothes for Zalmai when Aziza's ones were perfectly fine . . . and that ridiculous television that could get us killed.

RASHEED: My son will have the best.

LAILA: While the rest of us starve? Aziza is fading away before my eyes . . . her ribs are pushing through her skin . . . her calves are as thin as my arm. I can't bear it . . . I can't.

RASHEED: Well . . . I've decided we will send her out to beg . . .

LAILA: *(beat, incredulous)* No.

RASHEED: I wasn't asking.

LAILA: I don't care if you are or not.

RASHEED: I owe more than you know about and there is nothing left to pawn, your ring, the gun, everything of value is long gone . . . and you'd be amazed how much children can bring in . . . There are others like her . . . younger even . . . everyone in Kabul is doing the same.

LAILA: I don't care about everyone else.

RASHEED: I've made inquiries . . . there's a safe corner near the mosque.

LAILA: I won't let you turn my daughter into a street beggar.

RASHEED: I'm warning you, woman.

LAILA: You're the only one allowed to go out and get a job, so go out and get one.

RASHEED: *(incandescent with rage, takes everything he has not to go for her)* I swear you're going to make me kill you, Laila . . . I swear it . . .

Mariam, Aziza, and Zalmai enter and see the danger of the situation.

ZALMAI: Mammy?

Rasheed falls back, storms out.

LAILA: I'm okay, baby . . . I'm okay . . . Zalmai, bring me a glass of water . . . Aziza, it's okay . . .

They exit.

MARIAM: You shouldn't . . . you shouldn't provoke him . . .

LAILA: I know . . . but I can't help myself . . .

Choreographed sequence to denote passage of time. Kabul is becoming more and more like a wasteland; people are becoming more desperate.

SCENE FIVE

Aziza enters with a piece of cloth. She sits on the ground and spreads the cloth out in front of her. As she speaks, she places each item carefully in the center of the cloth. Mariam and Laila watch on, heartbroken.

AZIZA: My flowered shirt and my wool gloves, my doll, a pair of socks, my pumpkin-colored blanket with stars on it, and my set of dice . . .

MARIAM: Good, my love, everything is packed.

AZIZA: Tell me again.

LAILA: It's a special school where the children eat and sleep so they don't come home after class . . . This is to make sure that they can concentrate properly on their studies . . .

AZIZA: Do the students sleep alone in different rooms or together in big rooms?

LAILA: Together I would imagine.

AZIZA: And are the teachers nice?

LAILA: Of course, all teachers are nice, because they help you to learn.

AZIZA: And will I be able to make friends?

Laila, overcome for a moment, cannot answer. Mariam steps in and takes Aziza by the shoulders.

MARIAM: You are the most clever and most pretty girl I have ever met, everyone will want to be your friend, okay?

AZIZA: Okay . . . and how long do I have to stay?

LAILA: Not long, darling, not long at all.

Rasheed enters with Zalmai carrying their burqas.

RASHEED: Time to go.

The women take their burqas and begin to put them on.

LAILA: And if they ask about your father, then what do you say?

AZIZA: The Mujahideen killed him.

LAILA: Good . . . you understand why?

AZIZA: Because if I tell the truth, then they won't take me . . . it's a special school . . . *(Beat. She is solemn.)* I don't want to go.

LAILA: As soon as your father finds work we'll come and get you.

MARIAM: They have food there, rice and bread and water and maybe even meat.

AZIZA: But you won't be there, neither of you.

LAILA: I'll come and see you all the time. Look at me, Aziza. I'm your mother. Even if it kills me I will come and see you.

RASHEED: Come.

They walk in file across the stage until they reach the orphanage.

Zalmai and I will wait around the corner . . . *(Rasheed looks awkwardly at Aziza, a beat of guilt.)* Before I forget . . . *(He takes an apple from his pocket and hands it to her.)*

AZIZA: *(surprised)* Thank you.

Zalmai steps forward, throws his arms around Aziza.

ZALMAI: *(struggling with this, torturous for him to say)* Ziza . . . you can have my ball . . . if you like . . .

AZIZA: *(moved, fights back tears)* Oh, thank you, Zalmai . . . but you should keep it . . . I can't look after it like you can . . . be a good boy and I'll be home soon . . .

RASHEED: Zalmai, come.

Zaman enters. He's a bookish man, quite like Babi in nature and stature. He invites them to sit at his desk.

ZAMAN: So you are from Herat? My brother-in-law used to live there. He was a glassmaker. He made these beautiful jade-green swans. You held them up to sunlight and they glittered inside, like the glass was filled with tiny jewels. Have you been back?

MARIAM: No.

ZAMAN: I'm from Kandahar myself, oh, it's lovely, the gardens, the grapes, oh, the grapes . . . they bewitch the palate. But of course Herat is wonderful too, a city of artists and writers. You know the old saying, that you can't stretch a leg in Herat without poking a poet in the rear . . .

Aziza giggles.

Ah there . . . I made you laugh, little *hamshira*, that's usually the hard part. I thought I was going to have to cluck like a chicken or bray like a donkey, but there you are . . . and how lovely you are . . . perhaps your grandmother could take you outside a minute while we talk? *(Aziza panics.)*

MARIAM: It's okay, Aziza, we will be right outside, let's go.

They leave. Laila stares after them, then bows her head.

ZAMAN: I know this is not easy . . .

LAILA: I feel so ashamed . . . what kind of mother abandons her own child?

ZAMAN: This is not your fault . . . It's those savages who are to blame . . . and you are not alone, *hamshira* . . . we get mothers like you all the time . . . mothers who cannot feed their children because the Taliban won't let them go out and make a living. So you don't blame yourself. I understand . . . and I know this place is in a dire state . . . but we manage. Allah is good and kind, he provides. Aziza will be fed and clothed, and we will teach her something every day, covertly of course. All right? *(Laila nods.)* Now don't cry, *hamshira*, don't let her see you cry.

Mariam enters with Aziza, signals to Laila it's time to leave.

LAILA: God bless you . . .

Laila holds Aziza close, kisses her face, pulls herself away. Mariam and Laila go to exit. Aziza flies after them and is restrained gently by Zaman.

AZIZA: No! Mammy! Mammy! No! Khala Mariam!

Mariam and Laila exit as she cries, Mariam comforting Laila as they go. A choreographed scene as they cross the stage, encountering Talib soldiers as they go. Then Laila returns again alone. The Talib soldiers stop her, beat her; she keeps going, is stopped again. By the time she reaches home she is breathless.

SCENE SIX

Laila comes through and collapses over the kitchen table. Mariam moves forward to inspect her back.

MARIAM: Oh, Laila . . .

LAILA: Is it bad?

MARIAM: Bad enough . . . *(She starts to apply ointment.)* What did they beat you with?

LAILA: The first with a radio antenna, the second with a tree branch . . .

MARIAM: The second? You didn't come home after the first?

LAILA: Aziza is waiting for me, how could I come home?

MARIAM: They will kill you if you keep this up.

LAILA: I have to see her . . . Rasheed refuses to come at all . . . says he is too tired . . . that's a laugh . . . ahhhh.

MARIAM: Be still . . .

LAILA: Maybe tomorrow I should wear extra layers, padding from the beatings . . . *(Mariam shakes her head.)* I know you miss her too.

MARIAM: *(long beat, suffering in silence)* Yes . . . yes . . .

Aziza walks forward, in a dirty and basic uniform, hair pinned back neatly. She is different somehow, odd, as if pretending to be okay; she stammers slightly at times. Zalmai appears also, listening intently to her, ball under his arm.

AZIZA: There are fractures along the earth's crust called faults, and on the other side of them there are these sheets of rock . . . t . . . t . . . t . . . tect . . . t . . . t . . . tonic plates . . . and when they slide past each other they catch and slip . . . and it releases energy which t . . . t . . . travels to the earth's surface and makes it shake, and sometimes the shifting of rocks is deep, deep below and it's very powerful and scary down there, but all we feel up here on the surface is a slight t . . . t . . . tremor . . . only that . . . like a shiver . . .

MARIAM: You're getting so smart . . . much smarter than your dumb *khala*.

AZIZA: *(looks at her with affection, touches her face)* Oh, you're not dumb, Khala Mariam . . .

ZALMAI: Is Aziza coming home with us this time?

LAILA: Soon . . . very soon.

AZIZA: We've been learning reading and writing too, and geography and science and math . . . and we have balls of wool beneath our t . . . t . . . tables in case the T . . . T . . . Taliban come to inspect . . . we hide our books and pretend to knit.

MARIAM: And you are eating well?

AZIZA: Yes, eating well . . . we had lamb last night . . . or maybe it was last week . . .

MARIAM: And the other children are kind to you?

AZIZA: Yes, everyone is nice . . . *(A bell rings somewhere; Aziza desperate now.)* Don't go . . . stay a little longer.

ZALMAI: Baba has to go to work.

Aziza looks at Laila, confused.

AZIZA: He found work?

LAILA: He just started this week . . . a doorman in the hotel . . . he promises to bring you home as soon as he has some money saved up.

AZIZA: *(knows Rasheed will not bring her home)* Yes.

LAILA: He promises, Aziza . . . soon . . . very soon . . .

AZIZA: Yes, yes, of course . . . it's fine really, Mammy . . . I am fine . . . I am fine . . .

Aziza fades into the background; Mariam, Laila, and Zalmai walk home.

MARIAM: Did you notice? She stammers now.

LAILA: Yes . . . I noticed . . .

MARIAM: But she is learning so much, clever like her mother.

LAILA: Strong like her *khala* . . .

ZALMAI: I don't like that man.

Laila looks at Zalmai.

LAILA: What man?

ZALMAI: That man . . . standing at our door . . .

Laila looks up to see a man standing with his back to them.

MARIAM: Who is it?

LAILA: It can't be . . .

MARIAM: It can't be who?

Tariq turns.

TARIQ: Laila?

Laila flies into his arms; Zalmai comes behind, pulling her back.

ZALMAI: I don't like you. Mammy, tell him to go.

LAILA: This is just a friend, now go and play with Khala Mariam
in her room, okay?

ZALMAI: I don't want to.

LAILA: Zalmai . . . be a good boy . . .

ZALMAI: I want you to play with me.

LAILA: I won't be long . . . I'll tell your father to bring you home
some *jalebi* tomorrow . . . would you like that?

MARIAM: Come, that's a good boy.

*Mariam leads Zalmai off. Laila and Tariq stare at each other. Silence.
Tariq takes a small package from his pocket.*

TARIQ: Cheese . . . compliments of Alyona.

LAILA: Alyona . . . what a pretty name . . . your wife?

TARIQ: My goat . . . I had to tie her to a stake in the ground and build a fence . . . there are wolves where I live.

LAILA: And where is that?

TARIQ: In Pir Panjal in Pakistan, there's a wooded area nearby and pine trees. They mostly stick to the woods, the wolves, but a bleating goat . . . that can draw them out. It's a nice place, a summer retreat, hilly and green, lots of trees, high above sea level, cool in the summer. Perfect for tourists . . . you would like it there . . . *(This lands awkwardly between them; he looks away.)* Anyway, it's nice, a plain life, but I like it, I like living there . . .

LAILA: Just you and your goat?

TARIQ: *(smiles)* Yes . . . her fur is perfectly white; when it snows all night, all you can see is her eyes . . .

LAILA: I thought you were dead . . .

TARIQ: I've been gone a long time.

LAILA: No, Rasheed brought a man, he said you were dead, that he saw you, that you were dead.

TARIQ: I don't understand.

LAILA: Rasheed . . . he must have paid him . . .

TARIQ: *(sees she is upset)* Well, never mind . . . I'm here now . . . *(Beat.)* I'm so sorry about your parents.

LAILA: Thank you . . . and yours?

TARIQ: Also passed on . . . some years ago now.

LAILA: Oh, Tariq . . .

TARIQ: I went back to our old house, I thought I would meet some of our old neighbors, but I didn't recognize anyone.

LAILA: They are all gone.

TARIQ: I don't recognize Kabul either . . .

LAILA: Neither do I . . . and I never even left . . . though I wished I had a million times—

TARIQ: Maybe it was best that you stayed . . . the refugee camp in Peshawar was awful . . . a lot of people died, dysentery, TB, hunger . . . I saw so many children buried . . . There is nothing worse a person can see . . . *(Beat.)* The reason I didn't come before . . . *(He is ashamed.)* I was in prison, Laila . . .

LAILA: Prison?

TARIQ: A man paid me to take a leather coat to Lahore . . . *(Beat.)* I knew of course . . . that there was more to it . . . but we needed the money and I thought it was a risk worth taking . . . it wasn't. I never even got on the bus . . . it was in the seams, the hashish, spilled all over the street when the police cut it open. My mother tried to visit me in the prison, but they never let her in . . . *(Beat.)* It was a terrible place, Laila . . . terrible . . . mostly I wrote to you . . .

LAILA: You did?

TARIQ: Volumes . . . though I knew you would never receive them . . . *(Beat.)* But I kept writing them anyway . . . just in case. I spent seven years there . . . and then a friend told me about a job in a hotel in the mountains, and I needed to make some money to come and find you—

LAILA: I thought you were dead . . .

TARIQ: I know, you said, you don't have to explain. *(Tariq touches the bruising on Laila's face.)* Is he good to you? *(Laila turns her face away.)* If I had taken you with me . . . if I had made you come . . .

LAILA: Don't . . .

TARIQ: I know I went away and that you're married now . . . I'm not assuming anything and I don't want to turn your life upside down . . . if you want me to leave, I will . . . just say it.

LAILA: No . . . don't leave . . . please . . . please stay . . . listen to me . . . there was another reason I married Rasheed . . .

Lights up on Rasheed and Zalmai, sitting together, eating. Mariam serves food.

ZALMAI: Mammy has a new friend . . .

RASHEED: Does she now?

ZALMAI: He has a limp.

Mariam freezes. Lights dim on them as we return to Laila and Tariq.

TARIQ: Aziza . . . it's lovely.

LAILA: So is she . . . you will see . . . Rasheed works from noon

to eight . . . come back tomorrow afternoon and I'll take you
to her.

TARIQ: I'm not afraid of him, you know . . .

LAILA: I know, come back tomorrow.

TARIQ: And then?

LAILA: I don't know . . . I have to think . . .

TARIQ: I know, I'm sorry . . . I am so sorry for everything.

LAILA: Don't be . . . you promised you would come back and you
did . . . you did . . .

Tariq stands and goes. Rasheed looks up at Laila now, eerily calm.

RASHEED: Is it who I think it is?

MARIAM: He was just visiting.

RASHEED: Shut up, you . . . *(To Laila)* Well, what do you know . . .
two friends reunited . . . just like old times. So you let him in.
Here? In my house? You let him in here with my son?

LAILA: You tricked me. You lied to me. You had that man sit
across from me and . . . you knew I would leave if I thought he
was alive—

RASHEED: And you didn't lie to me? You think I didn't figure it
out? About your *harami*? You think I'm a fool? I suppose you
let him see your face?

ZALMAI: She did . . . you did, Mammy . . . I saw you.

RASHEED: *(to Zalmai)* Did you sit and talk with him too? *(Zalmai looks at Laila, worried now.)* I asked you a question, boy.

ZALMAI: I was upstairs, playing with Khala Mariam.

RASHEED: And your mother?

LAILA: It's all right, Zalmai . . . tell the truth.

ZALMAI: *(almost in tears)* She was . . . she was downstairs, talking
to that man.

RASHEED: I see . . . teamwork . . .

MARIAM: Rasheed . . .

RASHEED: No, no . . . it's too late, Mariam . . . it's too late. Zalmai, go outside.

ZALMAI: But Mammy—

RASHEED: Now!

*Zalmai goes. Rasheed stands and slowly removes his belt from his
trousers as he watches Laila.*

> After all I have done for you and your little bastard child . . .
> pulled you from the rubble, gave you a roof over your head,
> and fed and clothed you . . .

MARIAM: Please, Rasheed . . .

RASHEED: Took you in out of the goodness . . . the goodness of
my heart . . . and married you . . . all for what? So you could
throw it back in my face like some thieving lying whore?

Rasheed hits the table with his belt, making both women flinch.

MARIAM: Please . . .

RASHEED: *(to Mariam)* And you . . . *(Beat.)* After all these years
was it so easy to betray me? To see me humiliated in my own
home? In front of my son? *(His rage is growing by the second, he
moves toward Mariam with menace.)*

LAILA: Leave her be . . .

*Rasheed pulls Laila onto the table. Mariam claws at him, but Rasheed
pushes her off.*

RASHEED: Get off me . . . *(He launches on Laila again as she tries
to defend herself. He hits her with his belt, once, twice, three times.)*

MARIAM: Rasheed . . . stop . . . please stop . . .

*Rasheed ignores her. Mariam pulls her scarf from around her and puts
it about his head and begins to pull. He falls back, splutters and coughs,
frees himself, and turns on Mariam.*

RASHEED: This is what you wanted all along, isn't it? To turn
her against me? To force me to do this . . . you bitter . . .
twisted . . .

*Rasheed bears down on her now, punching and kicking until Laila
rises and grabs a glass and smashes it over his head. Rasheed lets out a
bear's roar and charges for Laila, smashing her down into the ground,
dragging her to the bed, where he places his hands around her neck and
chokes her. Behind on the floor, Mariam struggles to recover, to rise
from the floor and reach the spot where Rasheed is killing Laila.
Mariam watches on, frozen, terrified. Mariam panics now as she
watches Laila become weaker and weaker. Mariam looks about in desperation, seizing a shovel leaning somewhere. She grabs it with shaking hands, goes to stand in front of Rasheed. Laila falls limp now.
Mariam raises the shovel over Rasheed's head and brings it down with*

force. He stops instantly, falls forward, dead. A couple of long seconds pass and then we hear the desperate breathing of Laila gasping for air, her hands around her throat, as if she can't believe Rasheed's are no longer there. Mariam is panting also; she goes to Laila.

MARIAM: Are you okay? Laila? Are you okay?

Mariam helps her to sit up. Laila sees Rasheed, realizes he is dead, and becomes almost hysterical.

LAILA: Oh . . . oh, Mariam . . . what have you done? What have you done?

MARIAM: It's okay, Laila . . . it's okay.

LAILA: But you've . . .

MARIAM: Shhh, Laila . . . listen to me . . . *(She kneels before her, takes her face in her hands.)* We've got to move him before Zalmai sees him . . . do you understand? He can't see him like this, he can't . . .

Mariam gets up and starts to try to drag Rasheed. Laila is still sitting, shaking, trying to make sense of things, but she cannot.

Move, Laila . . . now . . .

Laila gets up and comes to Mariam. The two women, bruised and battered, start to drag Rasheed across the floor. Lights down.

A choreographed scene of the two women tending to each other's cuts and bruises. Mariam bandages Laila's wounds; Laila puts ointment on Mariam's cuts. There is a slow and beautiful grace to this, the calm after the storm. As Mariam tends to Laila, it's almost like a mother preparing a daughter for her wedding, washing and dressing her. When they are finished, they are kneeling, facing each other. Mariam speaks softly to her, calm and cool.

MARIAM: *(describes this like a beautiful dream)* Listen to me . . . we're going to leave this house and this city and this unforgiving country altogether . . . we're going to go somewhere remote and safe where no one will ever find us, where we can forget our past and find shelter, somewhere with trees, lots of trees, with a lake nearby where trout swim and where there are fields for the children to play in. We will make new lives, Laila . . . peaceful lives where we will be happy . . . finally happy . . .

LAILA: How?

MARIAM: There is a way.

ZALMAI: Baba?

MARIAM: Go to Zalmai. He needs you.

Mariam watches Laila move across the stage, lights down on her as we stay with Laila as she finds Zalmai lying on a bed, his arms wrapped tightly about his ball.

LAILA: Are you okay?

ZALMAI: Baba hasn't said my prayers with me.

LAILA: How about I say them with you tonight?

ZALMAI: You can't say them like he can.

LAILA: Well, I can try.

ZALMAI: Where is Baba?

LAILA: *(beat; the breath catches in her throat)* He has gone away.

ZALMAI: Where did he go?

LAILA: I don't know, my love.

ZALMAI: When is he coming back?

LAILA: I don't know.

ZALMAI: *(beat)* Did he leave because of me? Because of what I said about you and the man downstairs?

LAILA: It had nothing to do with you, nothing is your fault, now come and sleep . . .

Lights down on them and up on Mariam in her room; she sits on her bed. The reality of what she has done begins to sink in. She goes to the window, opens it. A nightingale begins to sing. Lights down.

SCENE SEVEN

The morning call to prayer. Mariam sits in the living room with a small paper package. Laila enters, dressed to leave, carrying two small bags.

LAILA: You're not ready?

MARIAM: I've prepared some lunch for you and Zalmai to take, some bread and dried figs and some cookies for Aziza. Take the bus to the orphanage and get her. Taxis are too conspicuous; you will get stopped for riding alone.

LAILA: *(shocked)* But what you said last night?

MARIAM: I meant it . . . I meant it for you, Laila . . .

LAILA: No . . . I don't want any of it without you . . . I want it to be just like you said . . . all of us going together . . . Tariq has a place in Pakistan . . . we can hide there for a while.

MARIAM: That's not possible.

LAILA: *(desperate now)* We'll take care of each other . . . as you said . . . no, I'll take care of you for a change . . . whatever you want I'll get it for you . . . don't do this, Mariam. Don't break Aziza's heart.

MARIAM: *(finding her strength again)* They chop off hands for stealing bread, what do you think they will do when they find a dead husband and two missing wives?

LAILA: No one will know, no one will find us.

MARIAM: They will, they are bloodhounds, and when they do . . . they will find you as guilty as me . . . Tariq too . . . I won't have the two of you living on the run, like fugitives. What will happen to your children if you are caught? Who will take care of them then? The Taliban? Think like a mother, Laila jo . . . *(Beat. There is a strength in her voice now.)* I am.

LAILA: It isn't fair.

MARIAM: But it is fair, it isn't right that I run. I have killed our husband. I have deprived your son of a father who adored him. How do I ever bring myself to look at him, Laila jo? How can I ever escape his grief? For me it ends here . . . *(Beat. Laila looks away, shaking her head.)* Look at me. *(Laila looks at her.)* There's nothing more I want. Everything I'd ever wished for as a little girl you and your children have already given me . . . *(Beat. She is resolved.)* Now kiss Aziza for me, tell her she is the *noor* of my eyes and the sultan of my heart. Will you do that for me?

Zalmai enters, dressed, rubbing sleep from his eyes, the precious ball beneath his arm. She turns to him, softer now, genuinely sorry.

You be a good strong boy now, you treat your mother well and look after your sister. *(She kisses him on the cheek, pushes down a wave of grief and guilt.)* I am so sorry, Zalmai jo . . .

She stands and takes Babi's book from somewhere and holds it out to Laila.

Go on . . . go . . . *(Laila takes the book, still staring at Mariam, urgent now.)* Go!

Laila takes Zalmai's hand and runs offstage. A Talib soldier comes forward and walks Mariam into the next scene.

SCENE EIGHT

Mariam waits in a small room with barred windows. The Talib stands nearby with a gun.

TALIB: Are you hungry, mother?

MARIAM: No, not hungry.

TALIB: I have a biscuit, it's good, you can have it if you like, I don't mind.

MARIAM: No. *Tashakor*, brother.

TALIB: Are you praying?

MARIAM: No, brother, I am thinking . . . *(Beat. We're not sure if she speaks these words aloud or is thinking them.)* I entered into this world a *harami*, unwanted, a weed . . . but I am leaving it as a person who has loved and been loved back . . . and maybe it is not so bad to die this way . . .

TALIB: Are you afraid, mother?

MARIAM: Yes, brother, I am very afraid . . .

A bell rings out and the Talib leads Mariam out into a large arena space. The bright daylight bears down; Mariam begins to pray.

You have created the heavens and the earth with the truth: You make the night cover the day and make the day overtake the night . . . and you have made the sun and the moon subservient . . . each one runs to an assigned term . . . now surely you are the mighty, the great forgiver.

TALIB: Stand there.

MARIAM: O my lord, forgive and have mercy, for you are the best of the merciful ones.

TALIB: Stand there, mother, and look down.

Mariam kneels, looks down. A long beat. And when the shot comes, Mariam looks up into the bright blinding light, released.

EPILOGUE

Birdsong. Sunlight through dappled trees. Mullah Faizullah, older now, and Laila, pregnant, holding a flower, walk through the woods. Tariq, Aziza, and Zalmai follow.

MULLAH FAIZULLAH: I was so very fond of Mariam, I was the one who sang *azan* in her ear when she was born. I was her tutor, yes, but I was also her friend . . . it nearly broke me when Jalil Khan gave her away . . . I'm so sorry to hear her life was full of such hardship.

LAILA: She had some happiness . . . she gave us much of it.

MULLAH FAIZULLAH: She must have. You've come a long way to see the place where she grew up . . . *(Beat.)* There used to be a stream here, but it's long since dried up . . . there's a path there now but the hill is steep. The light will be fading soon. I'll wait here, you go on . . .

LAILA: *(turning to Tariq)* I won't be long.

TARIQ: Take your time.

Laila walks until she finds the kolba. *She pauses in the space, trying at first to take it in and then to conjure up the place as it was when Mariam was a child. Inside the* kolba *there are broken bottles and leaves, weeds growing here and there. Laila breathes it in, trying to imagine Mariam there. She kneels and touches her hand to the ground, closes her eyes. A wave of grief passes through her.*

LAILA: *(recovers, smiles, touches her belly)* We spend hours wondering what to name the baby. Zalmai wants to call it Clark, after Superman . . . Tariq likes Mohammad and Aziza wants Omar . . . but we only ever suggest boys' names. Because if it is a girl . . . I have already named her . . .

Zalmai runs through and takes her hand.

ZALMAI: Mammy? Are you ready?

LAILA: *(takes one last look around, leaves the flowers on the ground)* Yes . . . I'm ready . . .

Laila takes Zalmai's hand and they move to join Tariq and Aziza. Together they begin to cross the stage, a refugee family moving toward an uncertain future. Lights down.